FROM PLAYSTATION® TO WORKSTATION

A Career Guide for Generation Text Surviving in a Baby Boomer World

Other Books By Suzanne Kleinberg

It's All About the Elizabeths: A Financial Guide for Canadian Teens

Employee Rights and Employer Wrongs: A Laymen's Guide to Your Rights in the Workplace

FROM PLAYSTATION® TO WORKSTATION

A Career Guide for Generation Text Surviving in a Baby Boomer World

Suzanne Kleinberg

Potential To Soar Publishing
Toronto, Canada

Canadian Cataloguing in Publication Data

Library and Archives Canada Cataloguing in Publication

Kleinberg, Suzanne, 1963-
    From Playstation® To Workstation : a Career Guide for Generation Text Surviving in a Baby Boomer world / Suzanne Kleinberg ; Michael Kreimeh, illustrator. --- 1st ed.

Includes index.
ISBN 978-0-9866684-0-1

    1. Job hunting. 2. Teenagers--Vocational guidance. 3. Young adults--Vocational guidance. I. Kreimeh, Michael, 1970- II. Title.

HF5382.7.K58 2010   650.140835   C2010-905213-7

Potential To Soar Publishing
Thornhill, Ontario

Printed in Canada

Dedication

This book is dedicated to Alia and Jamie who inspired me to write this book and to Michael Kreimeh who inspired me to finish this book.

Table of Contents

WII OR WORK 5

   EMPLOYMENT RESTRICTIONS 5

   START YOUR OWN BUSINESS 8

   WOULD YOU RATHER... 9

THE SEARCH BEGINS 13

   FINDING A JOB IN A HAYSTACK 15

   ATTITUDES TO LOOKING FOR WORK 15

   WHERE ARE THE JOBS? 16

   INTERNET AND YOUR JOB SEARCH 20

   SOCIAL MEDIA AND NETWORKING 23

   JOB SCAMS 33

BUILDING YOUR EFFECTIVE RÉSUMÉ 37

   WHAT IS A RÉSUMÉ? 37

   SKILLS 40

   INEXPERIENCE = EXPERIENCE? 45

   BASIC RÉSUMÉ COMPONENTS 47

   USES FOR A RÉSUMÉ 48

   HOW DO I BUILD MY RÉSUMÉ? 56

   SUMMARY OF QUALIFICATIONS 62

   EDUCATION SECTION 65

   EXPERIENCE SECTION 70

   SAMPLE RÉSUMÉS 71

   SELLING YOURSELF 77

   SELLING YOURSELF 77

   FUNCTIONAL VS. CHRONOLOGICAL 81

   HONOURS AND ACTIVITIES SECTION 92

JUDGE A RÉSUMÉ BY ITS COVER LETTER 107

   GENERAL CONSIDERATIONS AND TIPS 107

   WHAT DO I INCLUDE IN MY COVER LETTER HEADING? 113

   WHAT DO I INCLUDE IN MY INTRODUCTION? 115

   WHAT DO I INCLUDE IN MY BODY? 116

   WHAT DO I INCLUDE IN MY CLOSING? 118

   FORMATTING AND ORGANIZATION 119

THE SCREENING PROCESS 143

JOB APPLICATION FORMS 147

JOB INTERVIEWS 155

   EMPLOYER'S MARKET 155

   PREPARING FOR THE JOB INTERVIEW 159

   ANSWERING JOB INTERVIEW QUESTIONS 164

   ASKING QUESTIONS IN A JOB INTERVIEW 178

   NON-VERBAL COMMUNICATION 182

   PANEL INTERVIEWS 189

   DISASTROUS MOMENTS 190

   AFTER THE INTERVIEW 197

FROM WWII TO WII **203**

WHAT TO EXPECT ON THE JOB **215**

    Your Expectations as an Employee 216
    Your Employer's Expectations of you 217
    Learning the Corporate Culture 222

WORKING ABROAD **227**

VOLUNTEER WORK **229**

10 COMMON (YET WRONG) ASSUMPTIONS **233**

INDEX **237**

Introduction

"The people who get on in this world are the people who get up and look for the circumstances they want, and if they can't find them, make them."
- George Bernard Shaw

As anyone will tell you, today's job market is more competitive and difficult than ever to navigate. It's not the same as it was 20 years ago when most employers would take a chance on an applicant who didn't have all of the listed qualifications. It's becoming more and more challenging to conduct a successful job search; even more so for youth with limited experience and unpolished job searching skills.

So, are you now depressed? Discouraged? Stressed out? Well, don't be! The advantage that you have in today's job market is that you have more tools and resources available to you than ever before. You can access online job boards, digital newspapers, and social networking sites just to name a few to expose you to the resources that you need. You just need to know where to look and what to look for.

With the right preparation and strategy, you will have an advantage over your competition and be able to successfully develop your career. Through diligent practice on honing your job search, you will not be held back by the challenges and frustrations of progressing into the next phase of your life.

Through tips and exercises, this book will guide you through the tools that you'll need to land that crucial first step on the career ladder. Whether you are in Grade 8 looking for that first summer job or a recent University/College graduate looking for that first break, this book will help you understand what today's employers are looking for.

"The worst days of those who enjoy what they do, are better than the best days of those who don't."
- E. James Rohn

Preface

When I was ready for my first real job, I was repeatedly reminded to keep my résumé between 1 and 3 pages because that is all the reader will have time to read. And back then, that was the truth. Someone in Human Resources ("HR") would review your entire résumé, evaluate your skills and then either schedule an interview or mail you a rejection letter. And all jobs were posted in the local newspaper.

Times have changed from then (which was not that long ago). Now, the decision maker for the résumé is rarely HR. It is usually a Functional Manager (e.g. Help Desk Supervisor, Manager of Accounting, Web Development Manager, etc.) who has been insufficiently trained in basic hiring techniques. The manager is already overloaded with his/her daily responsibilities and has little time for a proper hiring practice. On average, s/he will make a decision on your fate within 30 seconds of reviewing your résumé.

So imagine being a student or a graduate looking for work. With only part-time, seasonal or no employment history, how does someone gain useful work experience? From speaking to many teens, young adults and their parents, I realized what a frustrating and disheartening experience this can be. This is a group of our society where expectations are high but support is low.

And yet, many educators to whom I have spoken admit that they do not include this material in their curriculum. The public education system is woefully underfunded to spend much time on the subject. Many of the colleges and universities feel that the prestige of their diploma is enough to launch a graduate's career. Others dedicate little time to this topic and it is usually taught by people who have not been active in the workforce for many years.

This is why I created this book. Not only does it contain numerous samples and explanations of the entire job search process, but there are exercises to reinforce the lessons. I hope it will fill a large gap in training youth to transition from school to successful employment.

Wii or Work

By the age of 13, many people are starting to look at securing part-time or summer work. Usually, your motivation is to get your hands on some cash to grow your video game collection rather than gain experience. Rest assured, both goals can be achieved. You're probably trying to figure out what's out there for you. Different ages present different opportunities.

Sure, if you have a university degree, you have an advantage to be considered for a job over other inexperienced youth. But, the reality is that you will most likely be faced with a frustrating situation especially if this is your first job. Most businesses do not want to hire "some kid" without experience, so even getting that initial opportunity is difficult. Plus, you need to be aware that the Federal and Provincial governments have strict codes outlining restrictions for employment for teens in regards to hours and type of work allowed. These restrictions can be a big deterrent for businesses so if you are a younger teen looking to earn some personal cash, you may need to look at different types of employment.

Employment Restrictions

(Please check your provincial website for more specific laws that pertain to you)

Teens 14-15 (or 14-16 in Manitoba)

During the school year:
- ✓ Restricted to 2-4 hours per day (depending on the province).
- ✓ No more than 20 hours per week.
- ✓ Work is restricted to no later than 9 pm.

Summer Jobs (no school).
- ✓ Up to 8 hours per day and no more than 40 hours per week.
- ✓ Work is restricted to no later than 10 pm (check your provincial regulations).

So, how can I get a job if:

✘ I have zero experience.

✘ I can't drive.

✘ I can only work limited hours due to federal and provincial law.

Let's look at some of the possibilities and how you can discover marketable skills you didn't realize you had.

Under age 14:

✓ You can work for your parents (if they own their business and it's not restricted by law for teens).

✓ You can have a paper route.

✓ If you live in a rural community, you can assist with farm work such as weeding crops, operating light machinery, sowing, harvesting, cleaning stables, or feeding animals.

✓ Perform odd-jobs for neighbours (cleaning garage, walking dog, babysit, wash car, paint fence, mowing lawn, etc.).

✓ Help at the community centre or church.

Restrictions:

✘ Can't work in a factory, construction site, industrial mining, venue that serves liquor, or in logging.

✘ Can't load a truck or drive a motor vehicle.

✘ Can't work in a commercial laundry or dry cleaning establishment.

✘ Can't work in any job that involves ladders or scaffolding (window cleaning, roofing, etc.).

Age 14-15:

✓ You can work in an office.

✓ You can work at a fast-food establishment (e.g. McDonald's, Tim Horton's, etc.).

✓ You can work in a restaurant (but cannot serve liquor).

✓ You can work in retail.

✓ You can work in a grocery store (stock shelves, bag groceries, etc.).

✓ You can work at a gas station.

✓ You can work in a cafe.

✓ You can work as a babysitter or pet sitter or dog walker.

✓ You can work on a golf course (caddy, retrieving golf balls, tidy locker rooms, etc.).

Restrictions:

Same as for the "Under 14" group.

<u>Age 16:</u>

At age sixteen, people can be hired at almost any place where an older adult can be hired. The only restrictions are that sixteen year olds cannot be hired for what is considered a hazardous occupation.

Unfortunately, some provinces consider operating a motor vehicle for a job as hazardous and therefore quash jobs such as delivering pizza or Chinese food. Aside from the positions listed above,

✓ You can work as a cashier or busboy or host/hostess at a restaurant.
✓ You can work at a retail store in stocking shelves or selling.
✓ You can work at a movie theatre.
✓ You can work at a hotel or resort in a domestic roles.
✓ You can work as a lifeguard (with the proper certification).
✓ You can work at a summer camp.
✓ You can work at a theme park or a fair (CNE, PNE, etc.).
✓ You can get work at the mall during the Christmas season.
✓ You can work at your local golf or tennis clubs.
✓ You can work at a day care.
✓ You can work at a plant and flower nursery or gardening centre.

Check out the student job bank online at **www.jobbank.gc.ca**. While this government site does not list all student jobs out there, it is a great start.

Start Your Own Business

So, if no one is willing to take a chance on you because of your youth and inexperience, what can you do? Why not start your own business? There are no age restrictions on starting a small business.   But do keep in mind the following:

- [ ] You need to able to promote your business to potential customers. Therefore, you need to feel at ease talking with people and being able to try to sell them something.
- [ ] You need to make a profit. You should ensure that the prices that you set are more than your costs.
- [ ] You need to remember that you need to satisfy your customer. Selling is only part of the business. If your customer is unhappy with your product or service, not only will they not come back to you for more, the poor word-of-mouth will spread. If you make your customers happy, they will supply you with contacts for more potential sales.
- [ ] If you do something wrong, regardless of whose fault, it can cause conflict, bad publicity or even a lawsuit. You should make sure that an adult is privy to what you are doing in your business. They can help you avoid these pitfalls or help you deal with them. If anything negative should happen, you must be prepared to deal with it immediately.
- [ ] Be prepared to work long hours. You really need to be committed in order to succeed as an entrepreneur.
- [ ] You need to be able to manage money including maintaining accurate bookkeeping, inventory and taxes.

So, what can a teen do to start one's own business aside from babysitting or a lemonade stand?

- [ ] Cleaning service (house, cars, garage, attics, basements, or pets).
- [ ] Yard maintenance (mowing lawns, weeding, raking leaves, shovelling snow, planting).
- [ ] Car Detailing (Monthly service to wash, wax, vacuum).
- [ ] Pet Sitting Service (pet walking, bathing, cleaning, feeding, taking care of pets while the owner is on vacation).
- [ ] PC tester/Website Developer/Computer Maintenance/Home Network Installation.
- [ ] Catering (cooking, baking).
- [ ] Painting (fences, gates, interiors, exteriors).
- [ ] Errand/Messenger/Concierge/Delivery service.
- [ ] Tutor (music, foreign language, math & science, computers, etc.).
- [ ] EBay/Online business.
- [ ] Freelancing (writing, drawing, photography).
- [ ] Pool cleaning.

Would You Rather...

Whether you are looking for a part-time or seasonal job or deciding on a career, you need to understand your strengths and preferences in order to be successful in your path. If you position your work towards a career that does not suit your personality (e.g. telemarketing jobs if you are shy), then your chances of being successful will be limited and, worse, you will be dissatisfied. The better you know yourself, the better your career choices.

If you are unsure about what the true elements of your personality are the strongest, try taking a personality test online. There are several free tests online. One such test can be found at **www.personaldna.com**.

As well you can investigate careers by accessing hundreds of profiles of occupational groups and interest quizzes at **www.jobfutures.ca**.

However, in terms of jobs, review this list of preferences to see what kind of career might be suitable for you. If you are unsure about the details of the role, then research it by doing a simple Google search. While this is not a complete list, it should inspire you to think about your direction.

Would you rather....?

People facing?	**Or On your own?**
Some jobs to consider: Trainer, Social Work, Food server, Customer service, Nurse, Coach, Salesperson, Receptionist, Cashier.	Some jobs to consider: Researcher, Programmer, Actuaries, Statistician, Forensics, Accounting, Writer, Illustrator.
Teamwork?	**Or Independent?**
Some jobs to consider: Performing Arts, Firefighter, Team Sports, Military, Consulting, IT Support, Child Care Worker, Flight Attendant.	Some jobs to consider: Researcher, Scientist, Bookkeeping, Lawyer, Doctor, Farmer, Entrepreneur, Painter, Mortician, Software Developer, Taxi Driver.
Manage responsibility?	**Or Minimal responsibility?**
Some jobs to consider: Event Planner, Lawyer, Management, Architect, Social Worker, Surgeon, Pilot, Air Traffic controllers, IT Server Administrator, Project Manager, Home Inspector, Paramedic.	Some jobs to consider: Ticket Agent, Custodian, Artist, Cashier, Bank Teller, Typist, Barista, Jewellery Designer, Clothing Salesperson, Movie Extra, Theatre Usher.

Outdoors?

Some jobs to consider: Camp Counsellor, Tour Director, Parks Management, Landscaping, Lifeguard, Pool Cleaning, Dog Walker, Forestry.

Or Indoors?

Some jobs to consider: Office Worker, Subway Worker, IT, Home Inspector, House Sitter, Website Developer.

Lifetime learning?

Some jobs to consider: Lawyer, IT, Medicine, Tax Accountant, Forensics, Computer Security Analyst.

Or Minimal Education Upgrade?

Some jobs to consider: Clerical, Cashier, COBOL/Mainframe Programmer, Some Teaching, Librarian, Construction.

Variety?

Some jobs to consider: Journalist, IT, Criminal Law, Paramedic Or Emergency Medical Personnel, Police, Firefighter.

Or Routine?

Some jobs to consider: Clerical Worker, Car Detailing, Fitness Instructor, Teacher/Tutor, Payroll Administrator, Cashier, Accounting, Dental Hygienist.

Travel?

Some jobs to consider: Pilot, Flight Attendant, Tour Guide, Sales, Property Risk Manager, Delivery Person, Truck/Tour Bus Driver, Performing Arts, Sales, Consultant, Motivational Speaker, Journalist.

Or Stationary?

Some jobs to consider: Office Worker, IT Help Desk, Bookkeeper, Principal, Economist, Dentist, Air Traffic Controllers, Car Mechanic, Hair Stylist, Legal Assistant.

Deliver Presentations?

Some jobs to consider: Advertising/ Marketing/ Sales, Trial Lawyer, Architect, Technical Specialist, Executive, Consultant.

Or Remain in the background?

Some jobs to consider: Accounting, IT Support, Clerical, Paralegal, Librarian.

Creative?

Some jobs to consider: Advertising/ Marketing/ Sales, Arts, Architect, Interior Design, Video Game Designer, Fashion Design, Makeup Artist, Performing Arts, Writer, Journalism, Animator, Editor, Copywriter, Graphic Design, Photographer, Landscaper, Event Planner.

Or Linear?

Some jobs to consider: Accounting, Paralegal, Corporate Lawyer, Book Editor, Manager, Trainer, Immigration Officer, Security Guard, Court Reporter, Secretary, Receptionist, Pharmacist.

Fast-paced?

Jobs to consider: IT Support, Broadcast Engineering, Paramedic, Firefighter, Police, Emergency Room Personnel, Athlete.

Or Steady paced?

Some jobs to consider: Legal Secretary, Teaching, Family Doctor, Travel Agent, Librarian, Human Resources Manager, Mortician.

Negotiator?

Some jobs to consider: Lawyer, Project Manager, Recruiter, Manager, Architect, Real Estate Agent, Sports Or Entertainment Agent, Entrepreneur.

Or No negotiation skills needed?

Some jobs to consider: Secretarial, Payroll Administrator, Trainer, IT Support, Nutritionist, Medical Technicians, Cashier.

Detail oriented?

Some jobs to consider: Surgeon, Finance, Engineering, Computer Support, Pilot, Business Analyst, Architect, Proof-Reader, Event Planner, Designer.

Or Big Picture?

Some jobs to consider: Project Manager, Executive, Economist, Retail Manager, Real Estate Developer, Politician, Department Manager.

People focused?

Some jobs to consider: Babysitter, Veterinarian, Pet Sitter, Home Care Worker, Nurse, Social Worker, Hygienist, Nutritionist, Charity Organizer, Medical Technician, Teacher, Speech Therapist.

Or Business focused?

Some jobs to consider: Process Improvement, Billings Administrator, Parking Enforcement, Collection Agent, Tax Inspector, Bankruptcy Lawyer, Telemarketers.

Stressful?

Some jobs to consider: Police, Firefighter, IT Support, Emergency Medicine, Air Traffic Controller, Stockbroker, Complaint Worker, Paramedic, Taxi Driver, Mayor, Astronaut.

Or Calm?

Some jobs to consider: Statistician, Mortician, Researcher, Hospital Administrator, Historian, Florist, Janitor, Forklift Operator, Musical Instrument Repairer, Actuary, Dietician, Bookkeeper, Barber, Jeweller.

❧Exercise: Match Up

We know that certain personality traits lead to a better fit in some jobs. Similarly, you should be aware of which personality characteristics define potential success in a job. Match up the occupation with the typical list of traits needed for success in that job. Keep in mind; while the list of traits does not encompass all the abilities that you would need for that job, it will give you an overview in order to know if it is a role worth pursuing.

<u>Job</u>	<u>Traits</u>
a) Accountant	1) Competitive, handles rejection, handle pressure, copes with instability.
b) Camp Counsellor	2) Detail oriented, needs little supervision, analytical, requires specific designation.
c) Cashier at McDonald's	3) Works shift work, good listening skills, can maintain physical inventory, selling skills.
d) IT Help Desk	4) Bachelor of Arts plus one year of college, patient, good communication skills, motivator, good presenter.
e) Clothing Store Manager	5) Subject matter expert, patient, good communication skills, enjoys one-on-one relationship.
f) Teacher	6) Patient, likes outdoors, adaptable, accepts supervision.
g) Telemarketer	7) Creative, good listening skills, good time management skills, deals with deadlines.
h) Graphic Designer	8) Motivator, customer service skills, accountable, good people manager.
i) Copywriter	9) Eye for detail, accountable, science education, can work independently.
j) Bartender	10) People facing, pleasant demeanour, able to do repetitive work accurately.
k) Tutor	11) Creative, self motivator, English or journalism degree.
l) Forensic Science Technician	12) Persuasive, can handle rejection, can deal with stress, shift work.
m) Actor	13) Can work in chaos, detail oriented, good listener, patient, problem solver.

The Search Begins

The Search for Jobs in Any Economy

If you look at the big picture of the job searching process, it is comparable to going to the hottest club in town with an exclusive VIP lounge. Your goal is to get past that velvet rope. But first you need to know how to get to the club, get past the door, and then, if you succeed, be welcomed into the VIP lounge.

<u>Job Posting</u>

When you see a job posting, it holds key information for you: what the company is, what the industry is and what the list of requirements are. You can compare this to knowing the club culture, the location of the club and the entrance requirements for the club (minimum age, dress code, cover charge, etc.). When you have the full information, you will be able to present yourself in a way that will appeal to the "gatekeeper" (i.e. bouncer, résumé reviewer). The gatekeeper's job is to keep out people who appear to be unsuitable. Without understanding the full requirements, you will never be able to package yourself to get past that front door.

Just as you want your clothes and grooming to present a favourable image of you, your résumé and cover email should be crafted to do the same.

Résumé and Cover Email

Your résumé and cover email is a way to present your qualifications to a potential employer to show them that you are an excellent match for the job and the company. Compare that with how you would show up at the club dressed in a manner that will get you noticed (in a positive way). You want to show how well you fit into the role while also demonstrating what sets you apart from your competition. Do you meet the company's/club's standards and image? How have you packaged your "assets" so that you get the gatekeeper's attention and convince him/her to let you in (in the case of a job, the sole goal of résumé is get you invited to an interview).

Interview

Good news! All that time that you took to prepare has paid off. You are one of the selected few allowed into the club/interview. Is that good enough? No, because your goal is to get invited into the VIP section which in our case is equivalent to being invited to join the company. Now you need to use your communication skills to present yourself as respectable, persuasive, charismatic and confident. This is where your communication skills will be the difference between success and disappointment.

The task here is twofold: ensure you're sending the message that the receiver wants to hear and ensure you're sending the message that the receiver can understand (i.e. in the receiver's language, not yours).

Job Offer

And now.... you've convinced the gatekeepers that you stand above the rest of the masses while ensuring that you will represent their establishment to their high standards. You got the job offer/entrance to the VIP. Congratulations!

Now let's review this process step by step.

Finding a Job In A Haystack

*"Life's real failure is when you do not realize how close you were
to success when you gave up." -- Anonymous*

When you are well armed with a realistic self evaluation, a fair idea of the current job market, and some well made decisions about the type of job you are looking for, you can head off in search of that job. However, before you get stuck into the skills necessary to win a job, let's look at your attitudes...

Attitudes to Looking For Work

Which of these words **describes you** as a job seeker?

Eager	Assertive	Scared	Apathetic
Anxious	Disciplined	Nervous	Self-Defeating
Creative	Over confident	Careful	Slack
Ambitious	Flexible	Timid	Uninspired
Smooth	Comical	Complaining	Depressed
Cheerful	Intelligent	Shy	Egotistical
Impulsive	Organized	Cowardly	Lazy
Hopeful	Easygoing	Overwhelmed	Bored
Deserving	Resourceful	Not worthy	Entitled

How many **hours per day** do you think you would spend:

- Reading job postings online or in the newspaper/trade magazines?
- Visiting firms and talking to people who might help you?
- At an employment agency?
- Attending a networking group?
- Doing volunteer work in that field?
- Making telephone calls?
- Preparing networking letters/emails and résumés?
- Doing other things such as ....?

As you may have already concluded from contemplating the questions above, looking for the right job can be a full time job in itself.

Where Are The Jobs?

Jobs might be posted at your high school or university. Or you might be able to find jobs in the classified section of your newspapers or online on job boards or Craigslist. You might even be able to get a job by contacting various companies directly to see if they have openings. But the greatest amount of jobs available can only be found through the hidden job market.

The hidden job market contains 80% of the available jobs out there. Companies will use online job boards, head-hunters and newspaper advertisements as a last resort when all other methods have failed them. Companies would prefer to fill a position from a qualified résumé they have on file or from a referral by an employee. What this means for you is that you need to understand what industry, roles and companies that you want to work in and then proactively seek them out. Waiting for the ideal opportunity to be posted will guarantee that you will miss out.

Connecting to the hidden job market requires **networking**. And at your age, you probably haven't had a chance yet to develop many professional contacts. But that's okay. Talk to your teachers, professors, parents, family members, friends' parents, or other adults you know. Many will know about unadvertised job opportunities that they can share with you. But you need to show the initiative and let them know that you're looking.

Employment Web sites or job boards can still help you find a job. Some specialized Web sites cater to helping teens and new graduates find part-time or seasonal jobs.

Some **recruitment agencies** will hire teens to fill part-time positions. If you're new to the workforce, you might be able to get a temporary position in the type of field you might like to work in as a career. But a lot of the time, recruitment agencies look for people with specific skills and a minimum of 2 years experience. It is advisable not to spend much time on directing your search efforts to recruitment agencies. Remember, they get paid by companies for filling current job openings not by finding jobs for candidates. **Don't ever pay a recruitment agency to find you a job. It is a far too common scam.**

Volunteer work can also lead to paid work. For example, one teen volunteered at her local humane society as a pet care giver (feeding, cleaning, and exercising the animals). She received on-the-job training and was able to get an inside look into how the shelter was run. After just one year of volunteering once or twice a week, she was offered a part-time job working in reception and assisting in obedience training classes. This happened because the regular staff saw what a dedicated volunteer she was and thought she might be a good fit when the job opening came up.

Sometimes a job opportunity will fall into your lap. Other times searching for a job can be hard. If it does become difficult, don't get frustrated. Keep working hard towards your goal of getting a job, and one day you will succeed.

Informational Meetings

Contact companies or organizations in the field that you are interested and request an **informational meeting**. These meetings are an opportunity for you to learn about what qualifications you need; how to get them and what a "day in the life" in that field is really like. Plus it is a great opportunity to get in front of a potential employer. You would be surprised how many professionals are willing to help someone trying to break into the business.

Conduct your own research on the company, key personnel and industry by reading industry magazines, attending conferences and joining various associations. Try to find the name of one or two people in the company that would work in your area of interest and contact them via email. These are some of the best networking opportunities.

For example, if you are interested in advertising, you might want to start reading Marketing Magazine to gain insight into the industry trends, companies gaining new accounts and key players. Once you have names of key personnel, you can phone or email them to request an informational meeting. If you have any type of connection or common link with a potential contact, then use it. Otherwise, you can be just as successful if you demonstrate that you have an occupational interest.

Below is a sample email for an informational meeting at a veterinary hospital:

Hello Mr. Molinaro,

Please allow me to introduce myself. I am currently a student at Sudbury Community College Veterinary Assistant Diploma program with excellent experience in training and caring for animals in one of the city's largest shelters as well as the local Petsmart Doggie Daycare Centre.

I would like to offer my services to Doncaster Animal Hospital. Prior to enrolling at Sudbury Community College, I passed the "CPR for Pets" and "Grooming Dogs and Cats" courses with exceptional marks. I have also taken the initiative and trained friends and family on First Aid for pets as I feel that many pet owners could be saved the cost and anxiety of a lengthy hospital stay for their beloved pet. As you are aware, proper care for animals not only involves attending to the grooming, nutrition and medical needs of the pet but also the dealing with their owners in an effective and sympathetic manner.

In addition, I am in the process of authoring an article for the local community paper on "How to Hire a Reliable Pet Sitter or Dog Walker" which will, hopefully, be published in a future edition. I have also actively campaigned on behalf of the OSPCA for amendments to the current animal rights legislation.

I am excited to think about the possibilities of our efforts together and the value that we can bring to your clientele. I am confident that my services would be useful to you.

I would love the opportunity to discuss our collaboration further. I will contact you within the next couple of weeks to confirm if your availability to meet with me.

Thank you for your consideration.

Regards,

Lisa Jamal
705.555-6937
lisajamal27@yahoo.ca

Start the letter/email with a formal salutation (i.e. Mr. Smith, Ms. Baxter, Mrs. Sharpe, etc.). Don't address the letter/email with the recipient's first name unless you are already on a first name basis with him/her.

If you look at the structure of the above email, it starts with an introduction to get the reader's attention. This is where you would put in the name of the person with whom you networked. As you can see from the email above, it can still be effective if you don't have a referral name to insert.

Then you should talk about what relatable skills you can bring to them in one or two paragraphs. It also helps to show that you have an understanding of the nature of their business. In this case, the last sentence in the second paragraph that starts with "As you are aware" is added to show that you not only have the technical abilities but you also understand that there is a requirement for effective customer service and communication skills as well. By addressing these "soft" skills, you will present yourself as a well-rounded person and, effectively, eliminate any potential competition that did not address these talents.

Ensure that you end the email with focus on the enthusiasm and value that you bring to the potential employer as well as a statement that tells the reader exactly what the next steps are. It is advisable that you state that you will contact them and what time frame. This statement usually motivates the reader to contact you.

Don't forget to attach your résumé to the email so that they can reference your background. They will be looking at this to determine whether you have the potential to work for them in the future. They may even have an opening that they have not posted publicly yet.

If you're very outgoing and especially motivated, you can initiate contact through a cold call asking for an informational interview. You will really need to rehearse your pitch thoroughly. You will not impress anyone when your discussion is filled with "ummms" and "errrs".

Develop a thick skin. There are going to be a lot of employers who will say no and that they don't need your services. Don't take the rejection personally. It's simply something that everyone who ever looks for a job experiences. Be positive and offer your services at a later date, if the potential employer ever needs it.

If you don't hear immediately from a company that you have contacted, feel free to follow-up to see if they received your request. Sometimes, people are just busy and they just need a reminder. Don't follow-up too frequently because you'll just become an annoyance. But polite follow-ups show that you're taking your job search seriously.

If you get an opportunity for an informational interview, show up prepared. Bring a printed copy of your résumé and a series of questions. Make sure that your questions are thoughtful and specific to the company to show that you made an effort in your research and that you have a genuine interest in this career field. Here are some possible questions to help you start:

- What educational requirements/professional designations would you recommend in order to be successful in this industry or role?
- What industry associations would you recommend I join?
- What do you see as the future of the industry within the next five years?
- What changes have you seen in your company/clients/role recently?
- What are the key characteristics that you look for in people just starting out?
- When is the busiest hiring time of the year?
- What would you suggest I do next in order to be hired by your company?
- If you aren't hiring right now for your division, would you recommend someone in another division who I could network with? Would you be willing to initiate an introduction on my behalf or may I reference your name?

Don't forget to use any opportunity in the discussion to sell yourself. Treat it like a real interview. (See "*Answering Job Interview Questions*" section later in this book for more information.)

Informational interviews are a great way to build your network and potentially be considered for jobs before they are advertised to the public. Don't forget to follow-up with your "network" every 4-6 months to remind them about your updated qualifications.

Internet and Your Job Search

Well there's no doubt at all that the Internet has made a big difference in the search for jobs online. There are now literally thousands, if not millions of jobs that are being advertised on a whole range of web sites all over the country and around the world.

But having all this information at your fingertips is **not** necessarily a good thing. Sure... it's great to be able to hit the databases of government and privately run job posting websites from the comfort of your own home provided you are aware of a few important things...

*It's very important that you use **ALL** the avenues available to you to find work - don't just rely on the Internet!*

While many employers and agencies do use the internet to find job applicants, many more continue to use traditional methods as well as (or even instead of) the internet.

When you apply for a job over the Internet, your application must stand out from the crowd if you are to be noticed.

Many job seekers are using the internet to find work, so you have lots of competition! And because employers and agencies use advanced technology (such as keyword scanning) to assist processing applications, you better ensure that each application is 100% perfect!

If you must use an email address at hotmail or some other free email site, please... **choose a sensible email address.**

What sort of impression does an email address of sexychickybabe@yourdomain.com make?

Here are more common problems with email addresses which can become costly job hunt disasters!

- Have you exceeded your email account quota or disk space allowed, with your ISP? If so, your mail will be bounced!

- Putting www in front of their email address -
  e.g. www.jennyt@hotmail.com The www. is (usually) reserved for web sites.

- Putting the wrong country code -
  e.g. jennyt@hotmail.com.ca is a totally different address and will never find you! Quite often this is happening with HOTMAIL accounts - e.g. there is NO hotmail.com.ca

- Omitting the country/domain code altogether - e.g. jennyt@hotmail just doesn't exist!

- Omitting the "dots" - e.g. jennyt@hotmailcom just doesn't exist. It is very easy to put the dots in the wrong place

- Using unprofessional names in your email address! You might think that it is funny to have "sexychickybabe@yourdomain.com" or slackerdude@yourdomain.com as your email address. But is this really the impression that you want to give to potential employees who don't know you? Keep the "funny" names for personal email.

You might think you can use the Internet to spam your generic job application out to 100's of employers/agencies via email! Short answer on that - DON'T! Employers can tell whether applications have been written *to* them specifically or whether they're a cookie-cutter broadcast letter.

Many companies have a web site. Make sure you check out the company web site before submitting your résumé. You might find some information which could improve your application such as past or upcoming projects, product information, charity involvement, company growth, etc. Or you might find you really don't want to work for that company at all (layoffs, mergers, questionable ethics, poor public image, restrictive corporate culture, etc.). It is certainly worth a look!

Scanning Résumés

To screen your résumé, an employer will most likely use a scanner. Your résumé will be scanned through an OCR (optical character reading) program used to read the text of your résumé and then store in a database. When an employer is ready to hire someone, s/he can search the database by specifying the type of experience, skills or education needed for a particular position. As well, they can eliminate a résumé that does not contain keywords from a job posting prior to any human reading your résumé.

This information is then used to sort all the résumés in the employer's databank. Any résumés that match are selected and printed. Key job titles, skills, areas of experience and education are some components that can be extremely important in having your résumé sorted and pulled from thousands of scanned résumés.

In other cases, if a large amount of résumés are received in response to a job posting, the company may have an intern or Executive Assistant ("EA") manually scan the applicants' résumés using the words listed in the posting. They will be familiar only with the keywords used and will not read any further into the résumé contents.

To ensure that your résumé is selected from a scan, you must include the key words that are likely to be used in the scanning process. One way to identify key words is to underline all the skills listed in ads and job descriptions for the types of jobs you want. Include these skills at the top of your résumé in a section like the one below. Most key words that employers sort by are nouns such as Accounting Manager. However, verbs such as "troubleshoot" or "calibrate" may be used to sort for some positions such as electronic technician. Ideally, you should try to incorporate keywords from at least 70% of the posting to make it past the scanner. (Of course, only if you have experience with these qualifications.)

KEY WORD SUMMARY
----
5 Years Customer Service Experience – Corporate Accounts
Internal Support – Staff Training – Procedures Development
Marketing – New Account Set-Up – Business Development
Credit Reports – Credit Approval – Collections
Computerized Systems, MS Word, Excel, Access, PowerPoint, MOSS

If an employer gives you the option of either submitting a scannable résumé by mail or by submitting a résumé by e-mail, always choose e-mail. Sending an e-mail résumé is better because e-mail is already in electronic, plain text format that database systems can readily accept - with no errors.

Job Websites

A popular way of finding a job is to post your résumé on a job posting website. By posting your résumé, you can:

- Apply for jobs posted on that site.
- Create an automated agent to notify you via email when a job that matches your criteria is posted.
- Be contacted by someone (usually a recruiter) who thinks your credentials would be a good fit for a job opening that they are looking to fill.

It is advisable that you post your résumé on as many legitimate sites that cover your area as possible.

Some sites that are recommended are:

Workopolis.com	Monster.ca	Careerbuilder.ca
Working.com	Hotjobs.ca	LinkedIn.com
Wowjobs.ca	Eluta.ca	SimplyHired.ca

The above sites are free to people wanting to post their résumé. You can also find jobs online by going to a corporation's website, Craigslist or a newspaper's website.

Social Media and Networking

Social Media (such as LinkedIn, Twitter, etc.) can be useful in your job search for two strong reasons:

1. Demonstrating your expertise

If you have limited experience in an industry of interest, then blogs or tweets can help you show your knowledge, interest and resourcefulness. You can create a simple twitter account or blog to comment on industry updates or articles. For example, if you are hoping to break into advertising but have little experience, tweet or blog about industry changes or current articles with your comment and a link to the main article. There are a lot of online resources to research material in almost every industry.

Samples:

> Did you see where SLICE picked up all of CHCH TV's US programming today? Makes you wonder...

> Industry Canada offering LMCS #wireless spectrum on first-come, first-served basis http://bit.ly/cEiUSG

> #banff2010: 3DTV believers invade Banff http://bit.ly/c3oIxq

This is a simple way to show that you are serious about a career in the industry.

If you are interested in becoming a graphic designer, programmer or other occupation that would require visual work samples, then create your own website and put the web link within your résumé or on your LinkedIn account.

Do not use your Facebook account!!! Facebook is not professional so you should avoid referencing your Facebook page. No employer needs to read the comments from your buddies or see your picture from your birthday celebration or calculate how many hours you play Farmville each day. As a matter of fact, some employers are doing searches on Facebook on job applicants as part of their background check so it is recommended that you either clean up your page or change your name on your account.

2. Networking

LinkedIn.com is currently the primary business social media out there. Firstly, it is a great opportunity to post your credentials. Recruiters do use this site to find appropriate candidates for jobs that are not posted. Secondly, LinkedIn also has a job board. Most importantly, LinkedIn has great opportunities to network with potential contacts. If you join groups of interest, you can see jobs, scheduled workshops or participate in discussions. You can even start a discussion if you need information about breaking into an industry or specific role. Once you are in group, you can see the members and their titles and link to them. Most people will accept your invitation and then you can contact them as part of your job searching network. You can even learn about many companies including some of their general statistics on their employee structure.

Newspaper Classified Abbreviations

Newspapers, including Canada Employment Weekly, and trade publications, such as Marketing Magazine, are still a source for job hunters although not as popular as they were 10 years ago. Many advertisers use abbreviations in their classified advertisements in newspapers for one purpose - *to save money.* The less space they use, the cheaper the advertisement will be.

The following list of abbreviations, *and their variations,* can be found in the Positions Vacant columns of most newspapers.

What do you think they might mean?

p.t. posn	avg. spd.	min. qual.
f. time	gd. hrs.	prom. oppty.
prev. exp. pref.	bckgd	trng. incl.
pd. wkly.	bldg. cnr. Smith & Brown Sts	intvw
approx 20hrs p.w.	stdnt.	asst. for P.R. Co.
sal. neg.	techncl. exp. nec.	a.h. work inv.
appship	perm. posn.	p.m. a.m
pls. ph.	temp. reqd	gen.
jun. trnee	ph. for appt.	clercl. off. duties
jun. typ.	char. refs. nec.	gen.
swbd., s/b.	bus. hrs., B/H	ph. ext.
w.p.m.	exper. essent..	Pers. dept.

What does this advertisement mean????

POSITION VACANT

Capable person reqd for perm posn in accounts dept. Prev exp in similar posn pref. Good s'hand essent and some typ exp reqd. We offer immed start in our lux off with excel conds. Sal neg to $18K. Ph 555 7669 x852 for appt during bus hrs. Refs nec.

Sounds a bit like latin, but in English it reads . . .

"Capable person required for permanent position in accounts department. Previous experience in similar position preferred. Good shorthand is essential and some typing experience required. We offer immediate start in our luxury office with excellent conditions. Salary negotiable (means - can be arranged) to $18,000. Telephone 555 7669 extension 852 for appointment during business hours. References will be necessary.

Interpreting Employment Classifieds

Read over the following selection of advertisements, or look over last Saturday's paper, and answer the questions.

Try to:

- Work out what any abbreviations used might mean.

- Find those advertisements which don't give enough details about the job - are any of these "suspicious" or are they just vague and unclear?

- Decide whether any advertisements use any "clever" features or lines to make you notice them, and the "interesting" job being offered. Are they reliable? How can you tell?

CLERK

We have two (2) posns available in our mod. off. No exp. necessary but some background in office duties an advantage. Please contact Mr B Barton by ph. After 9.00am to arrange an appoint.

SMITH & BROWN P/L
1 Queen Street
Toronto
Ph: XXX-XXXX

---

*CLERK/TYPIST

Something a little different. A position exists for a capable young person with common sense to join our Personal Hygiene Products/Health Care sales team.

The successful applicant will be a fun loving, thorough and conscientious person with an eye for detail, a good telephone manner and willingness to work with and for a variety of people.

Attractive salary is negotiable. Benefits include a flex working environment, 4 percent RRSP match, exc. Gen. vacation, & good public transport or parking.

Please fax your CV to Alfred Rice at XXX-XXXX before October 22nd 5p.m.

JUNIOR, 16 to 17

Finance industry req keen, intelligent ppl for junior duties. Willing to train successful applicants. Must be interested and quick. Pls ph Tania at XXX- XXXX or William at XXX-XXXX.

JUNIOR

Smart jnr person wanted to assist cutter in jean factory. Poss. of trng for right applicant. Perm posn. Excel wages and conds. Only reliable persons need apply. juniorrole@aol.ca

---

PUBLISHING – JUNIOR

Large publishing company located downtown requires a junior to work in the Acc. Dept. Duties include gen clercl. work and daily banking.
Oppty. for advancement. Apply by ph. to Ms Rose at XXX-XXXX
ext. XXX.

DISPATCH Hands, 2 reqd, Ideal for stdnt. Immed. start. No exp. nec. Apply via fax to G Felder XXX-XXXX before 10am Tues.

YOUTH to 19 yrs. Handyman's asst. Ph XXX-XXXX.

JUNIOR SALES/CASHIER

We are seeking an enthusiastic junior for our "Store at the Gallery ".

Age: 16 to 19 years
Hours: Monday to Friday
Good education essential

Experience in cashiering or sales an advantage but not essential.

The person we are looking for will be good with figures and willing to learn. Full training will be given. The position offers an opportunity to start a career in retail if you have enthusiasm and drive. Staff benefits include discounts and superannuation after qualifying period. Fax resume attn: Mrs. Grace XXX-XXXX .

GUYS/GIRLS. Weekend work avail. In collection. Pay nightly. Students welcome. Ph. XXX-XXXX.

---

*CARWASH HAND** Casual and Perm work avail. for energetic young people willing to pitch in and work. Plenty of opportunity for those with ambition and good car drivers. Apply in person to

SPARKLE WASHES
44 Muddie Street
Hamilton

If raining, apply first fine day.
Weekend workers welcome.

---

*TYPIST/JUNIOR**

Join a friendly team in an interesting office. Loads of variety. Full training. Open the door with your interest and enthusiasm. Call Janelle Bowen XXX-XXXX.

GLUTTON FOR PUNISHMENT REQUIRED
If you're the type who gets turned on by schlepping around 200lb equipment, enjoys being confined to a tiny cubicle phoning for appointments, loves rejection, then:

YOU'D PROBABLY MAKE A GOOD COPIER SALESMAN
You won't be paid until you've made a sale, but when you do, we offer 20 per cent commission and an agency arrangement which should earn you $80,000 per year.

Few Perks, Motivation, Hard Work and Big Income - they're all yours at:

XXXXXXXXXXXXXXXX

Look at the LAST advertisement. Do you think it is a good ad, or is it a bad one? Why?

❧ Exercise: Revealing Details

Using the previous advertisements marked **with an asterisk ("*")**, try to reveal the following details about each one:

- What age is asked for? Is it stated or did you have to guess it from other information?
- What experience is required? Is useful?
- What skills are needed?
- What type of personality would you need to do that job?
- Do you know EXACTLY what sort of work the applicant will be applying for?
- What other information is given? What can this tell you about the job or the workplace?
- Are any of these jobs a bit "suspicious"? How can you tell?
- How do you go about applying for each job?
- Which advertisement appeals to you most? Why does it? Why don't the others?
- Would you apply for any of these jobs? Why? Why not?

  And finally...

- Which of these advertisements actually *helps you to write your résumé and application* to suit the position being advertised?

Misleading Employment Advertising

Scenarios

These scenarios show just some of the ways in which people can use misleading advertising to dupe many hopeful job hunters.

Read them, and then look at the questions at the end...

Training provided!

"Junior to join our city team.
Bright and enthusiastic girl to enter the computer industry. Training provided.
Typing an advantage. Phone: 306.555.0001."

When Simone got to the interview she was told that they were recruiting for an SAP training course which would last for three weeks... and would *only* cost her $450... and they would help her locate a job with a leading computer firm when she finished the course.

Simone later heard from some of the women who completed the course that it was over crowded, there were not enough computers, teachers or books, and it was in a rundown, very unpleasant building. After completing the course, the women that did get jobs did so with no "help" from the firm, or from the great "diploma" they had earned.

Excellent pay!

The job advertisement said **"excellent pay"** and **"exciting career prospects"**. However, Nick soon found out that instead of getting any of those rewards, the job cost him plenty of worry and time.

After weeks of work, he'd only got about $40 from his commission on sales. His telemarketing success rate was lousy, and now he'd sold all he could to his family and friends. And he couldn't get back the $25 he'd paid out for their "Sales Kit" which was required for the job.

No experience necessary!

Marybeth was desperately looking for a job, so she decided to apply for one that she'd seen advertised regularly for the past few months, which asked for:

"attractive young ladies and
men for some occasional TV & modelling work.
Must be presentable. No experience
necessary. Phone..."

When she called, Marybeth asked if she had to pay out any money and was told that she wouldn't... so she went in for an interview. She was told of her "wonderful potential" and her "bright future", but naturally, she would have to pay an agency fee so that a portfolio of photographs could be prepared by them.

When Marybeth told them that a photographer friend would be able to do the photos for nothing, she was told that the agency could only find work for her if she paid them a "distribution fee" of $250. Marybeth decided not to part with her money.

Later, she learned from a newspaper that some of the people who, believing that they would get good job, had paid out between $50 and $400 to the agency. These people said that after the photographs were taken and the fees paid, they had never been contacted. Later visits and phone calls told these people that they had been ripped off - the offices were empty and the phones were disconnected.

Hidden potential!

When Rick answered an advertisement for a consultant's position, he was told that his "hidden potential" could be released by doing a training course (that's why the ad also said that no qualifications or experience were necessary).

He soon found out that the "course", carried out in a tiny office packed with other participants, was worth nothing! Even though it cost him a lot, there were no jobs. It turned out that the firm that advertised was receiving a commission for every person it referred to the training school.

Agency fee!

William was only looking for a seasonal job, and after getting nowhere answering ads out of the paper, decided to answer an ad from an employment agency.

Obviously a lot of other people had seen the same ad, and just after 9:00 am, the place was packed. When he eventually got to the head of the queue, he was asked to fill in a form, take it to room "B" and there, pay a $25 "fee".

Then he was told, *"now would you take a seat upstairs so that someone can interview you? Thank you."*

There were just as many people up there too. After what seemed like ages, and only a few people being interviewed, and thinking that to even go to the restroom would cost him his spot in the queue, William went back to room "B" to say *"I've changed my mind... could I please have my money back?" "Sorry but - your name's on our books and if something comes up, we'll give you a ring..."*

Well... something did come up - a few days later it was reported in the newspaper that the Fraud Squad busted the place, but had just missed getting the people behind a nationwide racket which had extracted $25 from many thousands of people over the last few years.

The Glamorous Life!

Julie was 17 when she finished high school, and had high expectations of doing a "useful" training course and getting a good job. She was very impressed by an advertisement which promised "a challenging job", "meeting lots of interesting people", and a "glamorous life".

The Executive Assistant course she took was very expensive and very short. The diploma she received was worthless as she was rejected by employers for not being properly trained and for being too young.

When she finally did get an assistant's job, she found out that it mainly involved taking messages, serving coffee and hours of filing for minimum wage. She now thinks that the "glamorous job" and "fabulous position" lines she sees in other advertisements are designed just to trap you into a life of drudgery and boredom!

Hidden job!

A common ploy is the "pay to find you a job" scam. This scam is most common lately if you have your résumé posted on a website such as Workopolis or Monster.ca. A "recruiter" will contact you and set up an appointment to meet with you to provide you an opportunity to help you find "hidden jobs" that only their Secret Database contains. They will give you a sales job on how marketable your résumé is and that you could be getting a high paying job through their help. Then they will offer their services for *only* $5,000 to $10,000.

Watch out for this scam. They will never find you a job and most of these companies have countless complaints against them at the Better Business Bureau.

NEVER pay someone to find you a job. A recruiter is always paid by the company that hires you.

Job Scams

Be careful when looking for jobs on the internet. It is easy to be fooled by people who know what you want to hear and use it to fleece you out of money.

As the saying goes, "If it looks too good to be true, it probably is." Whether you are searching for a new job through valid job boards such as Workopolis or Monster, keep in mind that the same technology that help you in your job search may be used by scam artists looking to lure innocent job seekers into dubious job "opportunities".

Here are some "popular" scams to avoid:

Money-Laundering Scams

Money launderers often create job descriptions that offer commissions or pay high daily salaries to process cheques on behalf of foreign nationals. If you heard of the Nigerian Prince email scam, then you should be familiar with this variation. They are recruiting local citizens to "process payments" or "transfer funds," because as foreign nationals, they can't do it themselves. Their communications often contain broken grammar but may include well-written prose copied from legitimate employers' postings. Here is an example of a money laundering scam hidden behind what appears to be an offer of employment:

Job Title: Finance Manager

Dear Sir/Madam:

Our firm has an opening for a FINANCE MANAGER position.

This will be a part-time/home based position and the applicant must have the following qualifications:
Be able to check your email several times a day.
Confident PC user (SW Package MS Office), mail programs, Internet.
Cell Phone
At least 18 years of age.

What we offer:
Generous salary - $5,000 per month
Social benefits and health care plan.
Free training.

More benefits:
You don't have to pay for anything to work for us
No selling.
This is not network marketing or MLM.
This is not a distributorship.

Reshipping Scams

Reshipping, or postal forwarding, scams typically require job seekers to receive stolen goods in their own homes -- often consumer electronics -- and then forward the packages, often to another country. The victim who falls for reshipping scams may be liable for shipping charges and even the cost of goods purchased online with stolen credit cards. Or worse, the victim may be charged with smuggling or theft.

Pre-pay/Work at Home Scams

Although there are real jobs working at home, many "offers" are not valid forms of employment and may have the simple goal of obtaining upfront cash investment from the victim. Using claims such as 'be your own boss' and 'make money quickly', Work at Home scams will not guarantee regular salaried employment and almost always require an "up-front" investment of money for products or instructions before explaining how the plan works.

Envelope stuffing is a classic example of a business that may not be for real. If you were the employer, why would you pay someone $1 or more to stuff an envelope when you could outsource the task to a mailing house for pennies apiece? And in this digital age, how "in demand" is stuffing envelopes?

At-home assembly work is also highly suspicious. If these companies were legit, why wouldn't they be using offshore labor at a fraction of the cost?

Medical billing or claims processing is another one to be wary of. Knowing the confidentiality required in handling patient medical information, why would any legitimate medical professional allow just anyone to handle private medical information. Most doctors will not outsource billing services to unknown individuals but rather to large, established companies whose workers are trained and employed on site.

The refund recovery business was once popular. The scammers offer to sell you software to track late and lost UPS and FedEx packages and assist the shippers' customers in obtaining refunds. The victim is stuck with useless software and no customers.

In general, beware of work-at-home employers who ask for your credit card information or money up front. Legitimate employers pay you for providing a service, not the other way around.

Job Offer Scams

A newer form of employment scam has arisen in which users are sent a bogus job offer, but are not asked to give over financial information. Instead, their personal information is harvested during the application process and then sold to third parties for a profit, or used for identity theft.

If you receive a job offer that you are unsure of, watch for these signals:

- Don't get involved with an employer that can't make its business plan perfectly clear to you or one that's willing to hire you without even a phone interview. Do your own research on any employer that makes you feel at all uneasy.

- Never put your Social Insurance Number (SIN) number, credit card number, bank account number or any type of sensitive personal identification data in your resume. You should never share any personal information with a prospective employer, even if they suggest that it is for a "routine background check," until you are confident that the employer and employment opportunity is legitimate.

- Do not participate in any transaction in which you are requested to transfer money to a prospective employer. Look out for the Work at Home employers who insist you to make an up-front investment.

- Be cautious when dealing with individuals/companies from outside your own country. Even if they appear to send you a link to a legitimate corporate website, verify that the link is real and truly pointing to that corporation's website and not a dummy one made to look like it.

Questions on misleading employment advertising:

- Can you think about phrases that would alert you to a rip-off ploy?

- Can you understand why it might be easy to "con" someone who is new to the job market, by saying that they "have great potential" or "have a terrific future"?

- What guidelines would you draw up which might help you or one of your friends from being ripped-off in this way? What things should you look out for?

- What should you do if you are a victim of one of these rip-offs?

It is now against the law in some provinces to include advertisements which involve "training" courses in the actual "Positions Vacant" section of the papers. Have a look in your local/major newspapers or online job boards and see if you can spot any "suspicious" advertisements which might be misleading.

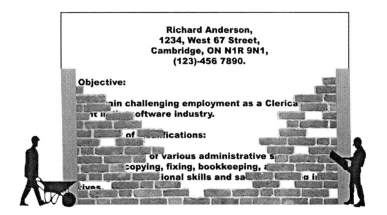

Building Your Effective Résumé

What Is A Résumé?

A résumé is a **concise** summary of your personal information, including such topics as your education, skills and qualifications that demonstrates your ability to be considered for the open position. When completed correctly, it can become an effective strategy document in your path to a fulfilling career.

John Q. Public
123 Avenue Road, Toronto, ON M1M 1M1
Tel: (416) 555-1234 Cell: (647) 555-4321 Email: John@public.com

Objective:

To gain more clinical experience prior to graduation through summer employment and/or a senior internship in the Oakville area.

Education:

2007-present   2nd Year Veterinary Student
University of Toronto

May 2007   Bachelor of Science, Animal Science, Pre-Vet Option
Minor: Chemistry
York University
Summa cum Laude, GPA 3.92

Summer Work Experience:

2007 Veterinary Assistant: Cat Hospital Veterinary Clinic, Mississauga, ON
Assisted three on-staff doctors with preparation for patient treatment, radiographs and surgeries. Aided with farm calls, preparation for and assistance in large animal surgeries, preventative care, and pregnancy confirmation.

2006 Veterinary Assistant: Lakeshore Vet Hospital, Etobicoke, ON
Demonstrated knowledge of technical competencies such as animal restraint, blood draws, processing of lab work, radiographs, and preparation of and assistance in surgery. Provided excellent patient care.

2005 Job Shadow: Lakeshore Vet Hospital, Etobicoke, ON
Prepared and assisted in surgery, restrained animals, took vitals and temperatures. Performed excellent patient care. Responsible for preparing prescriptions. Maintained professional appearance and cleanliness of clinic.

Volunteer Experience:

Toronto Humane Society – phone coverage and front office assistance, bathing and grooming
PetSmart – kennel duties, feeding and general nursing care.
Kemur Horse Center – grooming and hoof care, stall cleaning, feeding and watering.

Honours and Awards:

York University College of Veterinary Medicine Dean's List, Fall term 2006

Consider your résumé as a marketing tool that tells the hiring executive why s/he should take their valuable time to interview you. A résumé is not an exhaustive biography from the day you were born but a snapshot of relevant skills and experiences that demonstrate that you are an excellent fit for the position in which you are applying. Even if you have little experience, do not put unnecessary information in your document to pad it. Information that is irrelevant or too personal will guarantee that your résumé will swiftly end up in the garbage. Remember, the goal of your résumé is to get you an interview. This is its only true purpose and your goal at this stage.

Since the résumé is a professional document, look at the following exercise and see if you can guess which information you should consider to include in your résumé.

🖎 Exercise: Yes, No or Maybe

Indicate with a "Yes", "No", or "Maybe" whether you would include any of the personal features listed below, in a résumé.

- winning $20 in a hockey pool
- running a hockey pool
- playing in the local Soccer Competition
- pet sitting your neighbours' cats
- your First Aid Certificate
- your date of birth
- your religion
- subjects you are doing/have completed at school
- helping to organize the end of year dance
- your medical condition
- the 3rd prize you won in the local public speaking contest
- Whether you are single, married, separated, divorced, etc.
- working on the school yearbook
- names of good friends of the family
- reading comics
- the male chauvinist award given to you by the girls in your class
- your dreams of winning the lottery
- number of followers on Twitter

- your part-time job at Wimpy's Restaurant
- the committee you were a member of at your school/club
- where you went to Elementary school
- the fact that you haven't missed one episode of General Hospital in 10 years
- your country of birth
- the salary you would want
- your astrological sign
- your collection of U2 CDs
- being fired from your job at the local fish shop
- helping out at the local retirement home
- other languages that you speak
- your father's and/or your mother's occupation
- your email address
- having a paper route as a child
- your full address and telephone number
- the book you want to write some day
- any arrests or convictions
- car washing for charity

Skills

Often we think of "skills" as being unique or complicated special talents reserved for the highly trained or highly positioned. However, we all have certain skills which will be useful to employers.

There are the skills which you use every day but which you don't think about. Consider all the activities that you do on a daily basis (extra-curricular activities, taking care of your siblings, school projects, etc.).

It will be very useful for you if you can identify the particular skills you have now, or have the potential to develop, and can give examples of how you have successfully used that skill. Think about what challenges you have encountered and how you overcame those challenges to obtain the outcome.

Such information will help when you are writing your résumé or when you are answering questions in job interviews.

✍ Exercise: Skills Assessment

For each skill contained in these lists, state whether you:
- have that skill already (put a "✓")
- don't have it yet but have the potential to develop it (put a "?")
- will never have that skill (put an "X")

ALSO, think of appropriate examples of occasions where you have used that skill successfully.

PEOPLE SKILLS	INFO SKILLS	MATH SKILLS	MANUAL SKILLS
guiding	coordinating	counting	driving
listening to	confidentiality	calculating	operating
negotiating with	processing	timing	installing
instructing	collating	recording	lifting
supervising	keeping records	bookkeeping	repairing
understanding	prioritizing	compiling	adjusting
persuading	classifying	comparing	producing
speaking to	retrieving	problem solving	preparing
serving	copying	correcting	changing
helping	persuading	analyzing	adapting
nursing	planning	financial planning	creating
encouraging	typing	graphing	classifying
leading	proof reading	budgeting	using
motivating	editing	tracking	improving
responding to	composing	filing taxes	collecting
healing conflict with	teaching	estimating	handling money
make laugh	communicating	projecting	cooking
disciplining	writing	inventory tracking	selling
aiding in emergencies	reading	account balancing	programming
meeting with	imagining	bill paying	designing
assigning work to	adapting	investing	fundraising
directing	analyzing	money transferring	designing
evaluating	researching	foreign exchange	developing
coaching	compiling	estimating	organizing
counselling	comparing	forecasting	cleaning
being polite to	formatting	negotiating	managing
teaching/tutoring	proposal writing	cost/benefit analysis	assessing
mentoring	interpreting	credit management	building
presenting	publishing	inventory	assembling
telephone	marketing	purchasing	applying

Are there are any other skills that you can think of?

Examples of Your Skills

It is a good idea to keep some sort of list of your achievements, participation in special events, or any items that you may have made, which would be useful in your job applications. Then when you create a résumé for a specific job, you would apply an applicable achievement to demonstrate similar experience to the skills required.

For example: Writing a blog

How can use a personal hobby such as writing a blog about your favourite sports team or television show for your résumé? Let's list just a few of the skills required for blogging:

- ✓ Writing.
- ✓ Editing.
- ✓ Journalism.
- ✓ Research.
- ✓ Formatting.
- ✓ Proofreading.
- ✓ Communicating effectively and professionally.
- ✓ Managing a website including design updates, technology management and security implementation.
- ✓ Responding to reader comments and issues.
- ✓ Marketing/promoting your blog.
- ✓ Design of your blog.
- ✓ Responding to trends in content, design and/or technology.
- ✓ Monitoring your competition.
- ✓ Generating interest.
- ✓ Attracting and maintaining advertisers (if any).
- ✓ Balancing commitments.
- ✓ Originality and creativity.
- ✓ Planning design, topics or interactive activities with your readers.
- ✓ Understanding legalities of plagiarism slander and copyrights.
- ✓ Cost management.
- ✓ Coordinating, recruiting, hiring and/or supervision of other bloggers.
- ✓ Proficiency in publishing software and any upgrades.

These are just a few skills. You could probably add even more to this list.

✎ Exercise: How Would You Do This With....?

Now it is your turn to brainstorm. Review the list below and make a list of skills that you would practice or learn from each of the following achievements.

- Member of a dragon boat race team.
- A garden which you helped establish.
- An article published in a magazine.
- Your hand-made pottery.
- Taking part in a community organized forum.
- Act as curling team skip.
- A swimming trophy.
- Presidency of the local fellowship group.
- Making and modelling an article of clothing.
- Starring in a drama production.
- Helping the school librarian.
- Taking part in public speaking contests.
- Getting the prize for selling the most tickets in the school raffle.
- Volunteering at a food bank.
- Organizing a clothing drive.
- Help coaching your little sister's hockey team to a third place trophy.

Add any of your own special achievements, and write how you could present that achievement to an employer. When applying for jobs, it will help you if you can produce some evidence of what you have done, or what you are good at.

Exercise: What Skills Might You Need To Gain A(n):

Now, look at different job types and think about the skills that are needed to perform the job effectively. If you are unsure of the responsibilities of the role, feel free to research it on the internet. Once you are able to break down the skills, you can match them to your own abilities and experiences.

- Internship at an advertising agency (Art Director, Account Coordinator, Copywriter, etc.).
- Amusement park attendant or announcer.
- Trainee dress designer's job.
- Place in a creative writing course.
- Summer job as a receptionist in a law firm.
- Job as a cabinet maker.
- Employment as a gardener.
- Customer service representative.
- Graphic designer co-op student.
- Hair Washer at a salon.
- Pet Groomer's Assistant.
- Animal shelter volunteer.
- Community centre swimming class assistant.

As well, think about these questions:

Is there any need for caution when deciding what experience to discuss at an interview?

Is there really anything wrong with showing off what you are good at? Why? Why not?

Inexperience = Experience?

Some people who have not had a full-time career-focused job feel that they have little experience to offer. But if you recall past part time jobs or activities that you have participated in, you will be surprised at what experience you can offer.

✍Exercise: List Your Activities

Mark with a ✓ the things that you have ACTIVELY been involved in. If there are any other activities you get involved in, add them to the list as well.

☐ Paper route	☐ School council
☐ Child care	☐ Distributing pamphlets
☐ Organizing dances or events	☐ Essay competitions
☐ Scouts/Guides	☐ Running raffles
☐ Captain or coach sporting team	☐ School band/orchestra
☐ Debating	☐ Choir
☐ Library assistant	☐ Group leader
☐ Messenger	☐ Take-out food shop
☐ Public speaking	☐ Supermarket-cashier/bagger
☐ Gardening	☐ Selling raffle tickets
☐ Care of family	☐ Math competition
☐ Drama-acting	☐ Helping neighbours (provide examples)
☐ Drama-stage hand	☐ Helping parent's business or interests
☐ Drama-ticket sales	☐ Church/community groups
☐ Pet ownership	☐ Charity collections
☐ School clubs	☐ Language studies
☐ Computer repair for family/friends	☐ Community fundraising volunteer

When you have finished, try to identify which skills that you have learnt by being involved in that activity - use the following list as a suggestion (but there WILL be other skills not on the list):

☑ Money skills	☑ Organizing paperwork skills
☑ Organizing people skills	☑ Technical skills
☑ Helping people skills	☑ Physical skills
☑ Creative skills	☑ Reporting skills
☑ Communication skills	☑ Sales skills
☑ Number skills	☑ Responsibility skills

For example, a person running a paper route develops certain...

Physical skills	-	walking/biking up and down hills, pushing/pulling cart, delivering within 2 feet of door, bagging papers on rainy/snowy days.
Money skills	-	handling money and giving correct change.
Number skills	-	counting papers, counting change, tracking time.
Technical skills	-	maybe, when the chain falls off the bike and needs to be fixed?
Communication skills	-	talking to customers - you don't just say "Waddayawant?"
Organization skills	-	getting to work on time, completing deliveries on time, organizing papers in cart, timely delivery, etc.
Responsibility skills	-	deliveries on time and in good shape, addressing customer issues, collecting money.

... and more than likely many other skills as well!

Now try to summarize (in the list below) the special skills you may have learnt so that you can include them in your résumé. Remember HOW you learned those skills so that you can provide PROOF to a future employer!

Exercise: Ten Key Skills

1. ....

2. ....

3. ....

4. ....

5. ....

6. ....

7. ....

8. ....

9. ....

10. ....

Basic Résumé Components

Here are the basic components of a résumé. It contains only the basic information any employer expects. (When you draw up your résumé, make sure that it does NOT look exactly the same as this one... You'll be surprised how many people do...)

Try to put a LOT more of your own personality into it while remaining professional.

NAME
Full name. Your name should stand out by using the largest font on the résumé. Don't use nicknames unless you use the nickname in a professional setting, for example, you can use "Bob" instead of "Robert" but don't use "Stinky" if that is what your friends and family call you.

ADDRESS *
Full address, including postal code.
Not a requirement anymore especially if you email your résumé. You can keep it in if you need to use up space.

PHONE NUMBER
It should be in a digital format with area code (e.g. 604.555.1212). If you don't own a phone of your own, leave a "contact" number such as a friend or a relative who can pass on message to you. Do ensure that the answering message is professional. You don't want a potential employer hearing you sing a song that tells the caller to leave a message at the beep.

EDUCATIONAL DETAILS
List details of your latest educational qualifications. For recent students, list the results of your school diploma, your grade point average (if it is high) or your relevant subjects studied, etc. List any school academic prizes that you have won or special projects that you worked on.

OTHER COURSES
List the details of any further education - what, where, when. Any Technical or Business College courses? University studies and results? Any special certificates such as First Aid? Any special field trips that are related to the job which you are applying? (e.g., class trip to the morgue would be useful to include if you're applying to a hospital job.).

WORK EXPERIENCE
In this section, list the type of jobs performed and the location of all places you've worked at in your holidays, summers, part-time or casual, co-op/intern programs or any school Work Experience Program and when. You should also include any applicable volunteer experience related to the position for which you are applying.

INTERESTS AND HOBBIES
You may wish to list some of your leisure time activities to give the employer some idea of what you are like. Make sure that you don't list things about which you know very little - you may get caught! Don't say you like watching T.V., playing Halo or other equally "useless"

pastimes (at least to the employer). And do **not** list personal information such as you like tattoos, you are getting married, your girlfriend is a model, you go to religious services daily, etc.

Do mention any special skills you may have - good at public speaking, art, soccer team, etc. Try to pick those personal interests which may be relevant to the job you are applying for.

REFERENCES

It is recommended that you just list "References available upon request" making sure that you can supply them. Don't provide contact information until you have verified with your references that it is okay to do so. Being a reference can be an inconvenience if you apply for several jobs so be sure that you are interested in the job before you provide the list of references. If a potential employer requests references, you can supply the names and contact information on a nicely typed separate page titled "References".

Uses for a Résumé

The number one use of a résumé is to get you an interview. The answers to the following questions about résumés will give you some idea of how useful they can be:

Why can't this information just be included in a cover letter/email?

A cover letter needs to be short and to the point so to include the résumé in with the letter would make the letter into a short story. Sentences also need to be properly constructed for a letter, however, you can use point form with a résumé.

Why do you need a résumé?

The résumé contains ALL the essential information about you that an employer needs to know. If you don't have one, you will find it very difficult to communicate with employers when looking for work.

How and when can you use one?

A résumé is useful in so many ways. For example, it can be:

- Attached to an application letter or networking email.
- Left at an office after a personal visit.
- Help you remember important details when talking over the phone or in an interview.
- Given to friends and other people (your network) so they know your skills etc.
- Useful when filling in application forms since it contains all your "correct" details.
- Spare copies can be given to other people in a panel interview situation.

How can a résumé be useful to you in an interview?

See the third point above. There is nothing wrong with placing your résumé on the table in front of you and referring to it in an interview. Just don't make it appear that you are coming up with your responses by reading it intensely. And don't make it seem that you are unfamiliar with its contents. You have it in front of you to use as a cue sheet. You can start a response to an interview question with "As you can see under my experience under IBM....." and not "Oh I didn't know that!" or "Oh look at that!".

How could an employer use your résumé after the interview?

At any time, an employer can use your résumé to get your contact details, or to decide who to (not) interview for a position. As well, they can use it for a security/reference check to verify that you have worked at the places, dates and roles that you claim. You will notice that many interviewers will use your résumé to write their interview notes on so that all their information is kept in one place for later review.

How long should a résumé be: 1/2 page, 1 page, 2 pages, 2+ pages?

A résumé should be at least one page long depending on your experience.

As you progress through life and you gain more qualifications and experience, your résumé will lengthen. Don't cram it onto one page if it needs to go onto a second page. Blank space is more pleasing to the reader than a page crammed with words in small font!

However, do not exceed two pages at this point in your blossoming career. Only include information that is relevant to job and/or company which you are applying.

And, finally, don't try to fill space with graphics, a picture of yourself, or unprofessional fonts. Your résumé will make a quick trip to the trash can if you do so. Even if you are applying to a graphic design or art director type role, do not try to show your creativity in your résumé. You should create a separate portfolio or online website for that type of demonstration.

How can you change your résumé to suit a particular job? Would it be worth it?

It makes tremendous sense to tailor each copy of your résumé to suit the particular job you are applying for. As a matter of fact, it is expected by the employer.

Create a "master" copy of your résumé information on your computer that contains all the details of <u>everything</u> you have done. With each application, check out the particular requirements of the position, and edit the master copy to reflect those things thought to be important by the employer. Delete what is unnecessary to the position and/or the company which you are applying. You should be "creating" a new résumé for every job opening. It may sound like a hassle but it won't take that long once you have a thorough master set up.

You'll make their job easier and you will be noticed more in the "selection" stages (that's where they decide who does NOT get interviewed).

Let's look at some examples:

The résumé sample shown below does follow the basic résumé outline suggested. But, only a little bit of extra thought has been put into their résumé.

Name: **Louis J. Grant**
Address: 68 Smythe Street, Toronto, ON M1M 1M1
Telephone: 416.456.3356 (message only)
Education:
    Central High School, 1995
School Certificate Grades
    English 2   Mathematics 3
School Assessment Results
    Science 4   Geography 3
    Commerce 2   Family Studies 3
Special Skills:
    Typing course at Centennial College - tested at speed of 70 w.p.m.
    Can work basic office machinery - small switchboard, copier, calculator, etc.
Work Experience:
    Weekend Assistant at Pizza Pizza, Toronto, February to October, 1995
    School Work Experience - two weeks in September 1995 at Leon's Furniture as Clerical
Assistant
Interests and Hobbies:
    Participate in the local social tennis club.
    Enjoy reading home furnishing and decorating magazines.
References:
    Available upon request.

Some points about Louis' résumé are:

- Obviously this person doesn't have a phone, and they have made arrangements with a relative or friend to pass on a message for them (that's good!). Without a phone contact point, you make it difficult for (most) employers to get in touch with you quickly, so they won't bother at all!

- They have identified the special office skills they have already developed.

- The résumé is too crammed - there isn't enough use of blank space (between sections) to make reading easier.

- This person played with centering some headings in the Education section, while everything else is Left Justified (lined up to left hand side of page) and indented (or moved slightly in) from the left hand side. The centering just doesn't seem to fit in this situation.

- The person added the date that he graduated High School. It is usually recommended that unless you are a recent graduate or current student that this date is left off. The date can indicate your age and lead to age discrimination when the résumé is being reviewed.

The résumé sample shown below also follows the basic résumé outline suggested. However this time a lot of extra thought has been put into their résumé particularly with the layout.

PAT BOOTH
Ph: 647.555.1098   Email: patb1233@aol.ca

Address:

20 Bridge Road,
Toronto, ON M1M 1M1

Education:

Central High School, 2002 - 2005

English	Grade 3 School Certificate
Maths	Grade 2 School Certificate
Science	Grade 4 School Assessment
French	Grade 1 School Assessment
Art	Grade 2 School Assessment
Geography	Grade 4 School Assessment

Plus Proficiency Certificate in French 2005

Work Experience:

1. April 1995 to now, packer at Sobey's Food Mart, Thornhill

2. January 1994, holiday work at Shell Vaughan as driveway attendant

3. August 1995 - School Work Experience, two weeks at Sobey's Head Office

Interests and Hobbies:

I like most team sports and play with the Weston Junior Basketball Association.

I enjoy helping my brother in his pet shop at weekends.

I have assisted my neighbours with some renovations and landscaping.

References:

Available upon request.

Some points to note:

You can see how the addition of blank lines between sections improved the readability of this résumé.

The contact details centered at the top are impressive and easy to find! In this case, using the centering with left justified and indented text in the rest of the résumé does not present a problem for the reader.

The repetition of the words "School Certificate" and "School Assessment" in the Education section is a bit boring and tends to affect the overall look and feel of Pat's résumé.

Too much use of the word "I" in the "Interests and "Hobbies" section. Try to find another way to present this information either with bullet points or defining them as achievements.

Building on from the previous basic résumé samples, the structure in this example has been changed significantly. This time, the focus is on the skills the job seeker has developed since leaving school/college (and one would hope that are relevant to the particular job being applied for).

Jenny C Smart

Telephone: 519.555.5575
E-mail: jcsmart2010@gmail.com
Personal home page: http://www.jencsmart.com

CAREER OBJECTIVE

I am seeking to obtain a position where I can maximize my clerical, administrative and financial budgeting skills.

HIGHLIGHTS OF EXPERIENCE

I have developed a broad range of skills which suit the needs of many employers.
I am able to confidently carry out the duties you are seeking with a minimum of instruction.

PERSONAL SKILLS

Effective Communications/Customer Service/People Skills

- My major work experience has been in front desk/public contact positions and I am proficient in all duties associated with a front office situation.
- I have developed excellent interpersonal skills and effective communication skills.
- I am quite confident and friendly when meeting and assisting people on all levels and am able to provide them with a quality service.
- I am able to efficiently, courteously and tactfully handle clients either in person or over the telephone.

Clerical Skills/Organizational Skills

- I am proficient in all duties associated with an office environment, including dealing with customer enquiries, reception duties, collecting and handling money, expense account tracking, banking, filing, typing, etc.
- I can operate various types of telephone systems and office equipment.
- I have the good organizational skills essential to the smooth running of an office, including the ordering of office requirements.
- I have developed effective liaison skills to assist with the organization of, and communication of information, in relation to seminars, meetings etc.

Financial Budgeting

- I am experience at tracking expenses including expense accounts and credit card statements.
- I am proficient at creating and managing a budget for office expenses.

Computer Skills

- I have had experience with a variety of different computer programs and systems, including (on Windows XP) programs which record client details, rental/landlord accounts details, student records, and word processing (including Word 2003 & Excel 2003).
- I have some experience on Macintosh systems with database and word processing.
- I find I can pick up quite quickly on new procedures/ tasks as they are explained to me.

WORK HISTORY

April 2005 - now	**Casual Clerk Grade 1/2**	Department of Water Resources	City of Waterdown
June 2002 - March 2005	**Casual Reception, Banking, Office Duties, Library and Science assistant**	Various local high schools	including Walrus, Walker Wells, Hometown, John Cook, Lizard Park, Ashfield
February - June 2004	**Part time Liaison Assistant**	Market's Bizarre	City of Waterdown
May 1998 - March 2002	**Reception, Typing, Office Duties/Supervisor**	Weasel and Possum Real Estate	Cutley Wells

EDUCATION

Secretarial Studies Course, High Park Technical College, Toronto, 1998.
School Certificate, Central High School, Waterdown, ON , 1996-1998.

REFERENCES

Available upon request.

Some points to note:

Other useful changes you could make to this résumé format include:

Use of Action Words could have helped avoid starting sentences with "I" over and over again on the page.

Adding extra blank lines (white space) between sections.

Note that the address is not listed. This is fine in this digital age if you are going to submit the résumé via email or website.

Centering the introductory sections - contact details, career objective, highlights of experience.

Centering the various section headings.

Using achievements or specific experience to describe skills, for example,

"I have developed excellent interpersonal skills and effective communication skills by creating newsletters and giving presentations to company employees of all management levels."

Make the objective more company and job specific instead of it being generic.

If the job posting requested specific computer skills, make sure that they are included in the computer skills section.

Try using tables to align information such as computer skills to add more white space and direct the reader to that information.

How Do I Build My Résumé?

"God gives every bird its food, but He does not throw it into the nest. He does not unearth the good that the earth contains, but He puts it in our way, and gives us the means of getting it ourselves." - JG Holland

A résumé is a brief document that summarizes your education, employment history, and experiences that are relevant to your qualifications for a particular job for which you are applying. The purpose of a résumé (along with your cover letter) is to get an interview. Research has shown than it takes an average of ten (10) interviews to receive one (1) job offer, so your résumé needs to be persuasive and perfect. Given this, your résumé must be **reader-focused, confident** and **persuasive**.

The general purpose résumé usually contains four sections:

1. Contact

2. Education

3. Experience

4. Honours, activities, and achievements

Contact Section

Unlike other sections of your résumé, this section does not have a special heading like "Contact Information". Instead it simply lists the information below, at the top of the page:

✓ Your full name.

✓ Your e-mail address.

✓ Your address (optional especially if you email your résumé).

✓ Your phone number(s) (use digital format including area code XXX.XXX.XXXX).

✓ Your URL (recommended if you are a web developer or graphic designer). If you have a personal website that is used for just for fun then don't include it especially if it is not professional looking. Employers do not want to see your rant about the movie you saw last night or your vacation photos from Daytona Beach.

Of course, as with the rest of your résumé, you'll want to double-check that all the information you include is current and accurate. Mistyping your phone number could easily cost you an interview! Also, if you list an e-mail address, be sure to check your e-mail regularly or you may miss an important message. Make sure that you use an email address that is professional (i.e. hottie@hotmail.com is not a great email address for applying for a job).

Employers will probably look first and last at your contact information section, so it's well worth your time to make this section easy-to-read and appealing to the eye. Whatever design choices you make, try to coordinate them with the rest of your résumé. Here are some specific design options:

- ✓ Use page design strategies to present information in a usable format. For example, to help readers find desired information, you might place your name in a larger font size, center it, boldface it, or anything to make it stand out.

- ✓ You may want to add a graphic element such as a horizontal line to help section off your contact information. Make sure the visual does not distract from your textual information. And under no circumstances should pictures or clip art be used!! It is considered unprofessional and immature.

- ✓ Coordinate with your cover letter. One way to make your application documents a professional package is to match your cover letter and your résumé. You might do this by creating stationery or a letterhead in MS Word or Adobe for both documents. For instance, if you use two columns for your phone numbers and a double line on your résumé header, you might adapt it for the top of your cover letter as well. Make sure to use the same fonts (size also) for both documents.

Let's think…

About you…

What are the different ways you may be contacted? How do you prefer to be reached?

Type	List	Use on résumé?
Email(s): (Make sure your mailbox is not close to being full.)		Yes/No
Home phone/Cell phone:		Yes/No
Mailing address:		Yes/No
Fax number:		Yes/No
Website:		Yes/No
Facebook page: (not recommended)		Yes/No
Other:		Yes/No

About the company or organization…

Think about which means of contact would be most convenient for the company? Did the job posting make any specific requirements about which contact method they require?

Objective Statement

What is an Objective Statement?

The objective statement is a short section (usually 1-3 lines), often in the form of a sentence fragment, immediately below your contact information. It is an "at-a-glance" picture of you and your career interests to show how you would do the current role but also how you would fit in long term.

Why write an Objective Statement?

It is an opportunity to emphasize key qualifications, skills and/or goals for your fit for the role and the company which you are applying.

Examples:

- ✓ An internship allowing me to utilize my knowledge and expertise in different areas. Very vague. (What kind of internship?, What knowledge? What kinds of expertise? Which areas? How will you contribute to this company?)

- ✓ To obtain a position in a Fortune 500 company that will recognize my skills and encourage growth within the company. Yawn. Be specific.

- ✓ Management position in procurement where over 10 years of experience will add value to operations. Good statement. It is specific and highlights how your experience is a great fit.

Where should you place this section?

This section always goes below your contact information to clearly identify how you fit into the company and the open position. It is your marketing or "branding" statement to sell yourself to the reader.

How to build an objective statement

Your objective statement should answer the following questions:

- What position are you applying for?
- What are you main qualifications?
- What are your career goals?
- What is your professional identity or brand?
- How can you be of value to the company?

Avoid such trite phrases as: "seeking a chance for advancement," or "where my skills will be utilized," or "where I can further my career."

You should tailor your objective for each position /company that you apply for. Reflect on your overall qualifications and career goals and demonstrate how they're a fit but also unique.

✍ Exercise: Fill in the Brackets

Think about companies that interest you and /or jobs you would like to have. Fill in the table using your experience, skills and /or education to see if you can structure a strong objective statement.

Position / Company	Qualifications, Strengths, Skills, etc.

Now, write some objective statements and fill in the brackets from what you have brainstormed.

To utilize my [qualifications, strengths, or skills] as a [position title].

A position as a [position title] for [company] allowing me to develop my [qualifications, strengths, or skills].

An opportunity to [professional goal] in a [type of organization, work environment, or field] as a [position title] with emphasis in [areas of expertise].

Remember: the goal is to entice the receiver to read your résumé.

Summary of Qualifications

A Summary of Qualifications section (also known as a "Professional Profile") is sometimes used instead of an Objective statement to highlight your strongest experience that pertains to the job. If you are new to the job market (i.e. little to no experience), you might prefer to exclude this section and just stick with the Objective Statement.

What is a Summary of Qualifications section?

The Summary of Qualifications section provides highlights of information to the prospective employer. Short and targeted statements about your skills and character attract the reader into the résumé for more detailed information. If the potential employer spends less than a minute reading each résumé that s/he receives, the résumé with the most relevant information in a highly visible location is the most likely to get additional consideration.

Why write a Summary of Qualifications section?

Where you have a decent amount of experience, you may want to highlight them under the heading of "Summary of Qualifications" (also known as "Professional Profile") to list these attributes. The employer reviews your résumé` for 'highlights' of you skills. For instance, applying for an office job would require some skill in clerical duties.

Instead of saying, "I've worked in the clerical field for six years as a receptionist, data processor, and word processor," be creative and sound professional. Such as:

Administrative Support (6 yrs) – Responsibilities included answering the phones, data entry, and word processing for the CEO.

Your Summary of Qualifications should consist of a maximum of 4 major points. Use descriptive words and stay within 2 lines of content for each point. The best way to do this is to turn your job duties into a titled attribute. For instance, if you entered payables and invoiced customers you could create attribute titles like Accounting Clerk and Customer Service.

There are two formats you can use:

One way is to write this section in paragraph form. A qualifications statement can be a short paragraph usually no more than 4-5 lines long. Again, focus on what you believe will make the greatest positive impact on a prospective employer. You can do this successfully by focusing on what the employer needs, not what you think is interesting to you.

Example #1:

Proven ability to design and implement highly effective online marketing programs, outstanding project management skills, excellent ability to identify strategic opportunities and solutions, proactively manage a complex budget, with quarterly roll-ups to ensure spending matches to budget.

Another way to write this section is to use bullets. These statements do not need to be full sentences. There really is no preferred method of writing a qualifications statement with bullets.

Example #2:

- Proven ability to design and implement highly effective online marketing programs.
- Outstanding project management skills.
- Increased on-line sales of brand Z by 20% within first 6 months of taking over account.
- Streamlined order process to improve shipment efficiency by 25% and lower costs by 15%.

Each part of the summary of qualifications section should project an image of confidence, initiative, knowledge and success.

Where should you place this section?

This section will go at the top of your résumé under your contact information. If you use an Objective Statement as well as this section, then this section would go below the Objective Statement.

Note: You usually would not have both "Objective" and "Summary of Qualifications" sections on a résumé especially if you have strong work experience you wish to highlight. Remember, you only have about 30 seconds to get a busy reader's attention so you want to pick the statement that will do it. Choose which one would suit your résumé best.

How To Build Your Summary Of Qualifications Section

The next exercise will help you brainstorm how to develop content for this section.

✎Exercise: Highlights

Write down 3 or 4 points in your résumé that you would like to highlight from your experience for the following types of jobs. If you have any statistical data (e.g. decreased customer complaints by 15%, managed budgets over 50K, etc.) or any personal qualities (multi-tasking, customer service, etc.) then use them. Don't forget to include any pertinent educational achievements and /or technical skills.

Customer facing job (e.g. cashier, waiter, customer service, help desk technician)

_____

_____

_____

_____

Office clerical job (e.g. receptionist, database entry, refreshment service in meetings)

_____

_____

_____

_____

Camp Counsellor (e.g. day camp, sports camp, overnight camp, horse riding camp)

_____

_____

_____

_____

Education Section

Education sections vary tremendously on résumés - sometimes they are just a couple of lines while other times they span half a page. What's the best way for you to approach yours? Read below for some options.

What is an education section?

An education section highlights your relevant training whether it is school or other courses or certificates. If you have substantial work experience, this section may be very brief, simply listing the information below. If you are a currently enrolled college student or a recent graduate, however, you may want to build this section substantially.

The education section usually includes information about:

- Schools you have attended such as universities and / or professional and technical schools for university / college students or graduates (rarely high schools, unless somehow relevant or still in high school). As well, you should include any other relevant programs that you have enrolled or graduated.

- Location of schools.

- Date of graduation, actual or anticipated. *If you are not a recent graduate and have work experience, then do not include the date of graduation. This can lead to age discrimination.

- Degree(s)/Diploma(s)/Certificate(s) earned.

- Grade point average (GPA) if over 3.0. (Only for recent grads).

- Relevant seminars, workshops, self-study or webinars that you have taken regardless of length or venue of training.

Why write an education section?

- To persuade employers your educational background will help you do your job more effectively.

- To provide evidence of your qualifications.

- To highlight your areas of expertise.

- To display other learned skills that you can bring to the table that could enhance the requested skill set (i.e. French, accounting).

Where should you place this section?

Education sections, like experience sections, are usually placed in the middle of a résumé, somewhere between the objective statement and the honours and activities section.

If your educational background is your strongest qualification or may help your résumé stand out, then you'll probably want to put it near the top. Especially if you are a recent graduate, this section may be a major focus for recruiters. On the other hand, if your experience sections are stronger, then you'll probably want to move your education section below them.

How to build your education section

If you have the space on your résumé and/or if your educational background is particularly relevant, you may want to expand this section by including some of the content listed below as it applies to your experiences and career goals.

Simon Fraser University, Vancouver, BC. Candidate for B.A. in English, GPA 3.2. Focus: Professional Writing; Pre-Law. Expected to graduate in May 2011

Note: If you have enough information, you may wish to turn some of your content into subsections or even into separate sections. For example, if you know several relevant computer technologies, you might want to list them under the heading "Computer Proficiency" or "Technical Skills" rather than tuck them under your Education section.

Generally, you want to include your overall GPA, and even your major GPA and minor GPA. But if your GPA is below 3.0, you may not want to include it.

Samples
Major/Minor grade point average (GPA)
Major GPA: 2.9/4.0, Minor GPA: 3.1/4.0
Major and minor areas of study, concentrations, emphases or specializations
Minor: Management Information Systems
Concentration: Professional Writing
Emphasis in Individual and Family Development

Special projects
Special Course Project, Business Writing: determined feasibility of upgrading communication technologies in local business
Thesis: "Diversity Training in the Workplace"

Relevant coursework
Structured Programming Client/Server Computing
Object Oriented Programming
Local Area Networks
Familiar computer applications
Internet
E-mail, tele- and video-conferencing
Windows: Microsoft Office, XP, Vista, Windows 7
Macintosh OS X
Pagemaker
Photoshop
Dreamweaver
Quickbooks/ACCPAC/Simply Accounting
MS Excel – Advanced knowledge (e.g. Pivot tables, etc.)

<u>Continuing education courses, programs, training units, etc.</u>
Diversity or Management Training
Crisis Management
Academic honours or graduated with distinction
Summa Cum Laude - "with highest honour"
Magna Cum Laude - "with great honour"
Cum Laude - "with honour"
High School Award or Distinction
Certifications
First Aid Certification
Teacher Certification

Let's think...

What are the different educational or training experiences you have?

Types	List
What institutions, programs, schools, etc. have you attended?	
What educational training beyond traditional schooling and coursework have you had, if any?	
What language proficiencies do I have? (Spoken and/or written.)	
Any certifications or licenses? (CPR, Lifeguard, babysitter training, etc.)	
Do I have any on-the-job educational training such as in-house training programs? (e.g. managing cash, customer communications, etc.)	
With what computer programs am I most familiar or have taken training on?	

About the company or organization...

What can you expect the company to know about your degree program, coursework, training background, etc.? What might you need to describe or elaborate? Which non-traditional educational experiences would the company want to know about?

✒ Exercise: Education List

Make a list of all your education (including any courses, seminars, workshops, self-study or webinars whether it is related to your job skills or not) in the table below: See example listed

School	Diploma/Degree/ Designation/Certification	Key Courses	Dates
MacKenzie High School	High school diploma	Accounting Family Studies Advanced Algebra	2007-2010

Tailoring For Your Audience

To improve the effectiveness of your education section, you need to know what content will be most valued by the hiring company. By analyzing job postings as part of your job search, you can get a good sense for which educational qualifications are most desired.

You may tailor your education section in three main ways:

1. Select and include only your most relevant educational content:

    Based on your career goals and the required qualifications listed in job postings, you may choose to include or omit certain kinds of information. For example, if you earned a degree in a very specialized field (one that employers may need to know more about) or have taken specific courses directly relevant to the position, then you'll want to include a brief listing of coursework. However, if your degree is self-explanatory and employers likely will know your more specific credentials, then you may omit this detail.

2. Emphasize content through placement and design:

    Since the eye is drawn to section headings and the uppermost portion of sections, you may choose to put your most impressive and relevant educational experiences in either their own sections /subsections, or near the top of a section.

    For example, if you have substantial computer skills or have undertaken a special project, you may choose to put this information in its own section rather than simply list it beneath "Education".

3. List most relevant schooling first:

    While you may wish to use reverse chronological order (most recent schooling first), you also have the option of placing your most relevant educational experiences first.

Experience Section

Many job postings call for individuals with relevant experience and all employers will prefer experienced people to inexperienced ones. Your experience section can be the "heart" of your résumé as it will either open the door to an interview or lock it closed. How can you put your experiences in the best light?

What is an experience section?

An experience section emphasizes your past and present employment and /or your participation in relevant activities. Sometimes this section goes under other names such as the following:

- Work Experience.

- Professional Experience.

- Work History.

- Volunteer Work.

- Relevant Experience.

- Appointments / Co-op / Internship.

- Any activities that used the same duties or qualifications that may be used in the job that you're applying for.

Feel free to customize your headings for this section, especially if you are writing a tailored résumé. For example, if the job posting calls for someone with web development experience, you may want to create a section with the heading "Web Development Experience". Even the busiest reader will notice. Usually, résumé experience sections move from most recent to oldest experience. But with a tailored résumé, you may want to note important and applicable experience first, thus not following a chronological order (especially if you have limited experience).

Also, you may discover you need more than one section to organize your experiences. For instance, you may want a section for volunteer work and another for your work history or one for technical experience and another for supervisory experience.

The usual content for an experience section includes:

- Company or organization plus location.

  (Optional: If the company has a website, you can put in the link next to the company name. Reason: If the reader is not familiar with the company, s/he can get a quick glance from clicking the link).

- Position title.

- Dates of employment or involvement (MM/YY or YY).

- Descriptions of responsibilities and duties in the form of accomplishments, where possible. Accomplishments-focused descriptions tells employers how you've gone above and beyond in your jobs, what makes you special, how you've taken initiative and became an asset to the team.

<u>Sample</u>

Toyota of Canada Inc., Cambridge, Ontario. Security Officer, January 2007 to present
Assisted with loss prevention, access control, fire prevention, and emergency medical response.

However, you don't need to put all this information in this order. For example, if you wish to emphasize the jobs you held rather than the place of employment, you may want to list position titles first. Also, it is often much easier to read if the dates are aligned all the way on the right side margins. This way, it is easier to navigate through which experiences have been the most recent.

For the teen job seeker, you can make up for a lack of experience or qualifications with other activities that highlight your attributes. These activities could include volunteer work, sports achievements and educational courses in the appropriate areas.

Sample Résumés

The following pages demonstrate different types of résumé formats that can be used by teens or young adults with limited work experience.

SUZIE STUDENT

2833 E. 24th STREET, NORTH YORK, ON M4N 3N4
PHONE 416.555.3080 • E-MAIL: SUZIE.STUDENT@YAHOO.COM

OBJECTIVE
Seeking part-time Retail Sales Clerk/ Cashier position.

SUMMARY OF QUALIFICATIONS
- Customer-focused self-starter with proven client services skills.
- Energetic achiever and communicator, with strong listening skills.
- Quick learner, eager to learn and follow directions.
- Excellent team player who thrives in teamwork situations.
- Responsible and reliable with record of professionalism.

EDUCATION
- *High School Diploma*, Vanier High School, Toronto, ON, expected May 2007

HONORS AND DISTINCTIONS
- Earned Vanier High Advisory Council's Award for Academic Excellence, 2005-2006
- Achieved Honour Roll, Vanier High, 2005-2006
- Earned Certificate of Achievement for Outstanding Performance in Ontario Math Olympics, 2005
- Earned Varsity Letter, Vanier High Soccer Team, 2004-2006
- Earned Premier's Award for Educational Excellence, 2004

WORK HISTORY
Grocery Bagger, *Zehrs Supermarkets*, Wasaga Beach, ON, Summer 2006
- Prepared bagged groceries to customer specifications
- Assisted in loading groceries to customer vehicles
- Secured shopping carts and other key supplies
- Provided customer service to average of 60 customers per shift

Babysitter, *Suzie's Babysitting Services*, Toronto, ON, 2004 to present
- Maintained satisfied clientele of 10 families
- Provided quality care for children aged newborn to 12 years
- Managed all aspects of business

COMMUNITY SERVICE
- Supplied 80 community-service hours at Baycrest Retirement Community
- Donated more than 200 hours to Vanier Museum of Art, Fall 2005 and Spring, 2006
- Contributed more than 150 volunteer hours to Royal Ontario Museum Art Summer Camp, Summer 2006

SKILLS
- Computer literate in both Windows and Macintosh platforms
- Working knowledge of French, Portuguese and Italian

Christopher Tham

1234 Hickory Street, Chatham, ON K8K 5K4 | 519.555.5655 |
thamchris321@provider.com

Objective

I'm a high school student with great leadership skills and customer service experience who's looking for a challenging summer job.

Experience

Summer 2009 | A&C Logistics | Chatham, ON
Call Center Representative
- Provided excellent customer service in a high-volume call center.
- Handled highest call volume 2 months in a row.

2008-Present | Galt Collegiate Institute Student Council | Chatham, ON
Class Treasurer
- Planned quarterly social events for 2,000 students.
- Led school-wide food donation drive that collected 1,000 pounds of food for the local food bank.

Education

2007-Present | Galt Collegiate Institute | Chatham, ON

Maintaining a grade point average of 3.7

Active member of Student Council

Ontario Debate Regional Championship winner

AMBER L. MOFFAT

519.555.6565   amberlm2000@aol.ca

QUALIFICATIONS

Academically-gifted student who excels at math and creative writing. Recently achieved score of 1600 in Ontario Math Olympics securing 3rd place in the Provincial competition with additional honours as Class of 2010 Valedictorian. Self-published book of children's short stories which has sold 50 copies to date. Consistently displays leadership abilities as Manager of Christmas Program for the Kiwanis Boys and Girls Club of Regent Park, Toronto. Motivational communicator capable of building harmony and collaboration across all levels of team members.

ACADEMICS

YORK MILLS COLLEGIATE INSTITUTE, Don Mills, ON
High School Diploma, Expected June 2010

- *Student Council Treasurer, 2009-2010*
- *Valedictorian, 2010*
- *Finalist, Ontario Math Olympics, 2010*
- *Member, Dragon Boat Club, 2009-2010*
- *Captain, Tennis Team, 2010*
- *President, Poetry Club, 2009-2010*
- *Member, French Club 2008-2010*

ETIENNE BRULÉ SECONDARY SCHOOL FOR FRENCH IMMERSION, Toronto, ON
Coursework, *Summer 2009*

- Studied French immersion in both verbal and written.
- Participated in two week residency in Québec City.

UNIVERSITY OF TORONTO SCARBOROUGH CAMPUS, Scarborough, ON
Coursework, Summer 2008

- Attended bootcamp program for Advanced Writing Skills for Talented Youth Program

PROFESSIONAL EXPERIENCE

RICHMOND HILL GOLF & COUNTRY CLUB, Richmond Hill, ON   2006 and 2007
Assistant Tennis Pro (Summers)

- Gave individual and group instruction to club members and their children.
- Assisted in selling tennis products in the pro shop including clothing, rackets, shoes and visors.
- Maintained equipment and premises.

Alia Jordan

123 Rue University, Montreal, QC N5N 8N8
514.555.555 email: aliajordan@myschool.edu

OBJECTIVE: To utilize my copywriting experience and training to obtain an entry-level position as a copywriter at Cossette Advertising, Montreal.

EDUCATION:
Bachelor of Arts, Advertising, Degree anticipated May 2010
McGill University, Montreal, Quebec
Current GPA 3.53

EXPERIENCE:

Summer Intern, June 2009 to August 2009
ABC Communications, Montreal, QC www.abc.info

- Partnered with design intern to create and execute two sell sheets, one print ad and one postcard
- Created and presented collaborative intern campaign to entire agency and founders of organization
- Awarded best campaign of competing teams
- Wrote radio script submitted with campaign proposal and assisted in other writing assignments

Shift Supervisor / Trained Barista, September 2008 to present
Coffee Shop, Montreal, QC   www.coffeeshop.net

- Trained new employees, opened and closed store, handled total sales, built satisfied customer relationships

Server, Hostess, Expeditor, **Busser**, May 2007 to January 2008
Tremblant Restaurant, Montreal, QC   www.tremblant.ca

- Created customer base and close relationships with patrons of restaurant
- Provided prompt service while taking orders, serving food and closing the check

AWARDS AND ACHIEVEMENTS

- Dean's List - Spring 2008, Fall 2009
- Awarded best advertising campaign proposal for A Foundation, ABC Communications, Summer 2009
- Awarded best advertising campaign proposal for Health & Wellness Committee, McGill University, Spring 2008

COMMUNITY SERVICE

Newsletter Editor, Mount Royal Cat Rescue	2008 – 2010
Fundraising Letter Copywriter, Canadian Cancer Society	2007 – 2009
Fundraiser, Canadian Humane Society	2007

Selling Yourself

The more experience you have, the easier it is to sell yourself more powerfully. Since the recipient will dedicate only 30 seconds to each résumé before he / she decides if you are a fit, you will need to create a quick positive impact.

Look at the following résumé. The crucial elements that will sell you will be in the first half of the first page. You will see these elements at a high level in order to attract the reader in this area. This is the key section that you will be adapting for each job and /or company that you apply to. That is why it is important to review the job posting and company website thoroughly to understand what they are looking for in a candidate in order to make these sections compelling.

Quick Profile

The paragraph at the top is a brief overview of the Summary of Qualifications. Do not go into great detail. It is not a chronological summary of your experience nor is it a story. Don't use "I" excessively. The information can be in short form statements as long as the point is getting across to the reader.

Notable Expertise

This section is a series of bullet points of keywords of your experience and skills that either match the job description or are relevant to the job/company that you are applying to. For example, if you are applying to be a dog walker, you do not need to highlight your skills in Accounts Payable or your Visual Basic programming. However, you may want to highlight pet ownership, organization skills, or first aid training. Do not use more than 10 nor less than 4 bullet points. If you are applying to a job posting, use the same terminology used in the ad (obviously only if you have that skill or experience). Using the same wording will make reading (and decision making) easier for the reader.

Technology

This section is optional and used to highlight special skills that would be relevant to the job. You don't have to list software. You can list concepts such as content management, contract administration or CPR. Again, it is vital that the skill is relevant to the position that you are pursuing.

Awards / Work Status / Languages / etc.

You can add other high level information that you believe will be attractive to an employer. Any awards that you may have received that show excellence, dedication, hard work or teamwork are great to showcase. You would also create a separate section on the second page to list your awards to go into greater detail. These awards can be work, school or community related.

The "Work Status" listing is only used if you can work legally in another country outside of the one where you are seeking employment. For example, if you only have the legal ability to work in Canada, then *don't* use this line. If you are eligible to get a visa to work in the U.S. but don't have the visa, *don't* use this line. If you have newly immigrated to Canada and have a Canadian working visa, then *don't* use this line as it is assumed that you are legally able to work here. Only use this line if you have dual citizenship in which one country is Canada and/or if you have a valid visa to work outside of Canada.

Fluency in any language other than English is valuable even if the job does not require it. If you are fully fluent in a language other than English, then you would use the "Language" line. Otherwise, don't add this line.

Links

If you have your own web page, twitter or blog that is mostly business related, then list it. If you don't have one of those, then I would encourage you to set one up. Blogs and twitter accounts are great to enhance your résumé where you lack experience. For example, if you are trying to break into the media industry, you may want to blog or tweet about an industry article that you have recently read and provide a link. This shows a potential employer that you have knowledge about the industry and you are resourceful enough to research it on your own.

LinkedIn

If you don't have a LinkedIn account then you should create one. Go to www.linkedin.com and set yourself up once you have completed your résumé. Use the Groups to network and find out information on the industry or companies that interest you. (See "Social Media" section in this book for more detail.)

Facebook

Do <u>not</u> use your Facebook account as a link. Employers will not be impressed with your party pictures, wall-to-wall discussion with your best drinking buddy or hours playing Mafia Wars. Some employers are now searching Facebook to see the activity of potential employees so you should consider keeping your account clean or changing your account name. Even if you do not put your Facebook account as a link on your résumé, employers are using software search tools to investigate job applicants.

David Brandaware

Cell: 416-555-8251   Email: dave_brandaware@gmail.ca

Production and broadcasting experience on state of the art equipment. Completing degree in broadcasting from the College of Sports Media. Owner of freelance video production company, Dynamic Art Productions. Experienced in production and live event filming and editing. Proficient at set up of studio lights, cameras, microphones and sets as well as experienced in directing productions in fast-paced sports events and news / documentary reporting environment. I thrive in stressful and challenging environments while motivating my co-workers. I see a job through to the end regardless of the difficulties encountered.

NOTABLE EXPERTISE

- Excellent sense of visual composition, movement and perspective.
- Effective communication skills.
- Demonstrated sensitivity while working with crew and artists.
- Cameraman on two Toronto Rock live events
- Electronically inclined

- Physically capable of production lifting, camera assembly and lighting work.
- Proven ability to blend creativity with technical skills.
- Successful set up of lighting, microphones, and camera equipment for Michael "Pinball" Clemons lecture
- Audio mixing and wireless sound recording
- Production lighting design and setup

Technology Skills: Proficient at using Avid editing software, Burli software, lighting, microphones, webcasting, HD format and control room operations.
Languages: English, French, some spoken and written German
Work status: Dual Canadian and U.S. Citizenship, 101 Work Visa for U.K.
Awards: Best New Editor Award, Teamwork Award, Honour Society, Dean's List

www.linkedin.com/1211424324
www.myprofessionalwebsite.com/work_samples
www.myblog.com
www.twitter.com/davaware

Camera Operator/Editor   2009-2010
Bite TV www.bite.ca
- Wrote & directed a pilot called "In Your Face" a show that deals with issues in sports medicine.
- Acted as Camera Operator in ENG style shooting in unique places around Toronto.
- Directed several student films involving outdoor and indoor environments.
- Edited several live events over a very tight schedule for airing the same day.
- Managed the schedule of several edit suites by implementing a booking process that lowered editor downtime by 20%.

Camera Operator   2009-2010
Rogers TV http://www.rogerstv.com/
- Acted as Camera Operator on First Local News on 35 broadcasts.
- Taped various sports events with a reporter (ENG) on location.
- Recorded 16 OHA hockey games

Camera Operator/Live University Sporting Events   2008-2010
University of Toronto, York University and Ryerson University
- Shot basketball, hockey, football and soccer college events.
- Set up and broadcast live webcasting
- Assisted in cabling and wiring of the arena for live sporting events.
- Connected all cameras to the control room using fibre optic cabling.

PRODUCTION CREDITS

Editor, "History of the Marlies", LeafsTV	2010
Editor, "The Sports of Your Life", RogersTV	2010
Camera Operator, OHA Hockey Games, YRTV	2010
Camera Operator, First Local News, RogersTV	2010
Camera Operator, "In Your Face" – BiteTV	2009
Camera Operator, UofT Track and Field games, CP24	2009
Camera Operator, Ryerson University Varsity Games, CITYTV	2009

AWARDS

Best New Editor, Student Filmakers of Canada, "The Sports of Your Life"	2010
Teamwork Award, The Learning Partnership	2009
Dean's List, Seneca College	2007
Honour's Society, Westmount Collegiate	2004 -- 2006

EDUCATION

College of Sports Media, Broadcasting Degree, graduating early June   2010

Seneca College Kick Start Program   2007
- Successfully completed workshops on communication skills, conflict resolution, customer service, problem solving, and goal setting.

PUBLIC SERVICE

Paws for Cause Fundraising	2009
Canadian Cancer Society 10K Run for the Cure	2008
Kiwanis Boys & Girls Club Xmas Program	2005 -- 2009

Functional vs. Chronological

There are two popular formats for résumés: functional and chronological. It is recommended that you choose one of the two that is most suitable to the qualifications that you are trying to convey. It is not recommended that you tinker with either of these formats. People who read résumés don't want to have to figure out where the relevant information resides on your application. Creativity in résumé writing in terms of format is usually seen as someone who has difficulty fitting in.

Functional

In the functional résumé, experiences are divided into sections of expertise instead of former employers. This format is suitable for new graduates, candidates with limited work experience, and applicants with mixed unrelated work backgrounds. The target of the functional résumé is to stress specific key qualifications which have been demonstrated through a variety of work-related accomplishments.

The distinct feature of this format is that your skills are not ordered by date but by importance and relevance to the current job being applied for. It gives emphasis on the applicant's compatibility to the position being sought. A functional résumé permits candidates to align their accomplishments from previous work positions to create a more effective impact, since these skills might be spread out or go unnoticed in traditional résumé. Functional résumés also minimize the chance of you being asked about a lack of experience, frequent job changes and any gaps in employment history.

Stan M. Rosen
1001 Bathurst Street • Hamilton, ON N1N 1N1 • (519) 555-2345

Objective: Graphic Designer

Summary
- Experienced with design concepts for packaging and advertising.
- Photographer with skills in evaluating prints for reproduction.
- Understanding of video shooting and editing for television.
- Experience in Photoshop, QuarkXpress, Persuasion, PageMaker, Illustrator, Maker Pro, and MS Word.

Experience

GRAPHIC DESIGN
- Created consumer packaging using PMS and four-color processing.
- Produced ad campaign strategies for a variety of products and services.
  - Designed thumbnails, roughs, and final comps for print advertising.
  - Wrote copy for television and print media.
- Communicated corporate identity through design of logo and collateral.
- Created mechanicals; proofed blue lines and color keys.
- Used a wide range of typography to appeal to specific audiences.

PHOTOGRAPHY
- Photographed fashion and food compositions in studio settings.
- Developed portfolio of color landscape prints from across Canada
- Exhibited photos in two Ontario locations.
- Won award in black and white community photo contest.
- Experienced with black and white darkroom and other technical experience.

Relevant Work History
(Concurrent with Education)

2007-pres.   Freelance Computer Graphic Designer, Hamilton

2004-07   Marketing & Graphics Assistant, Baxter & Co., Burlington, ON

Education
B.F.A., Graphic Design & Marketing, anticipated Spring 2011

Ontario College of Art & Design, Toronto, CA

Marketing Program, summer 2006

York University, Toronto, ON

— Portfolio Available —

Chronological

For job seekers with solid experience and a logical job history, the chronological résumé is the most effective. Career changers and those who lack formal on-the-job experience (like new graduates) find this résumé the most difficult to write.

A chronological résumé starts by listing your work history, with the most recent position listed first. Your jobs are listed in reverse chronological order with your current or most recent job first. Employers typically prefer this type of résumé because it's easy to see what jobs you have held as well as when and where you have worked at them.

Paul Collins
6 Pine Street, Sudbury, ON K1K 1K1
555.555.5555 (home)   566.486.2222 (cell)
pacollins@gmail.com

Experience

Store Manager, Urban Coast Clothing   **April 2007 - February 2009**
- Managed and trained 10 personnel.
- Placed orders to restock merchandise and handled receiving of products.
- Managed payroll, scheduling, reports, email, inventory, and maintained clientele records.
- Integrated new register functions.
- Worked extensively with visual standards and merchandising high-ticket items.

Sales Associate, HBC - Children's and Teen's Departments   **July 2005 - April 2007**
- Merchandised children's and teen's wear.
- Set-up trunk shows and attended clinics for new incoming fashion lines.
- Worked with tailors and seamstresses for fittings.
- Scheduled private shopping appointments with high-end customers.

Bartender, Kelsey's   **February 2004 - July 2006**
- Provided customer service in fast-paced bar atmosphere.
- Maintained and restocked inventory.
- Experienced with various administrative responsibilities included closing register, processing work hour and tip information for payroll.

Education

Humber College, Etobicoke, Ontario
Humber Business Marketing Management Diploma   **June 2006**

Computer Skills

- Proficient with Microsoft Word, Excel, and PowerPoint, and Access

✍Exercise: List your work experience

List <u>all</u> of your work experience (including volunteer work) and activities that you have performed in each role whether they were part of your job or not. Include skills learned. See examples below.

Company	Position	Activities	Skills Learned	Dates
McDonalds	Customer Service	- Fulfill customer orders in busy environment. - Prepare food including special orders. - Take orders for drive-thru. - Replenish condiment section. - Clean tables and counters regularly. - Clean bathrooms.	- Customer service - Food preparation - Quality assurance - Teamwork - Money skills - Maintain cleanliness standards per health code. - Stress management - Multi-tasking	2007-2009
Smith and Smyth Law Firm	Filing Clerk	- File important client legal documents - Database entry in SAP application - Collect and input lawyer billable fees to the applicable dockets. - Managed petty cash. - Acted as relief receptionist during lunch breaks. - Managed busy Meridian switchboard. - Set up Executive and Client meetings. - Coordinated same day and overnight deliveries.	- Organization of important documents - SAP database entry - Timely accounts receivables. - Money skills - Customer service - Technical knowledge (SAP, Meridian switchboard) - Meeting room setup - Communication skills with clients and executives - Delivery management.	2006
Bill's Landscaping	Lawn mower	- Mowed lawns for residential and corporate clients. - Used various landscaping apparatus including John Deere tractors, power mowers, cultivators, seeders, sprayers and diggers - Deployed seed and pesticides - Installed sod. - Planted flowers and garden decor	- Customer service - Landscape design - Chemical management - Physical labour in various weather conditions - Flower bed arrangement - Plant/flower types and requirements - Operated and maintained equipment.	2004

Worksheet

Company	Position	Activities	Skills Learned	Dates

Why write an experience section?

- To convince employers that your experiences match their needs and corporate culture and you will fulfill their job requirements effectively.

- To provide evidence of your qualifications.

- To list and describe your experiences in the most relevant way applicable to the position you are applying for.

- To make yourself stand out and show what makes you unique.

Where should you place the experience section?

Most people put their experience section somewhere in the middle of the page, between their education section and their activities. If you have significant experiences, you may wish to emphasize them by placing your experience section closer to the top of your page. If your experiences are not obviously relevant, you may want to put your experience section beneath your stronger sections. For example, place it under your activities / leadership section.

Let's think…

Why you?

- What past and present experiences do you have - including not only jobs you've held but also positions as a volunteer, intern, student, leadership role, etc.?

- What types of experiences are generally desirable in your field or area of interest?

- Which of your experiences are most related to your career goals? How can you "sell" some of your seemingly irrelevant experiences?

About the company or organization.

- Which experiences are most desired by the company (as listed in job ads and position descriptions)? Which experiences would the company likely see as assets?

- Which experiences would contribute the most to the position for which you are applying?

Be sure to state the accomplishments of your experience. Use numbers such as:
- Deployed new computer hardware to 500 users.
- Created new process that reduced duplicate billing errors by 43%.
- Worked on event committee with budget of $45,000.
- Presented proposal in front of 2000 shareholders.
- Negotiated new contract resulting in $40,000 in savings.

Lastly, you may not have a lot of experience that pertains directly to the role to which you are applying. Don't panic! In these cases, setting up experience sections with two subcategories (responsibilities and skills learned) can help you communicate skills learned that are applicable to future positions:

Experience

Urban Outfitters, Toronto, ON
Sales Associate   December 2007 - Present

Responsibilities
- Conducted sales transactions
- Interacted with customers
- Tracked inventory and stock shelves
- Ensured store was clean and stock was organized
- Assisted with store promotions and displays

Skills Learned
- Interpersonal communication
- Marketing and sales
- Money transactions
- Following directions
- Working in a professional retail environment

While you may not think that the retail work you perform carries much value, the skills you're learning apply to a number of positions in a wide variety of organizations. For example, the interpersonal skills you learn dealing with irate customers during the Christmas rush can help you in stressful professional settings. Similarly for a job at McDonald's. While you are unlikely to zoom into a Vice-Presidency immediately after a summer stint as a cashier at McDonald's, there are a large amount of skills from that job that you can highlight on your résumé such as customer service, food preparation and handling money, just to begin with.

Action Words

Using action words, such as those listed below, at the beginning of sentences describe something you have done. The use of action words helps you avoid starting too many sentences with "I". Few things give a worse impression because "I" can make you sound very self-absorbed!

Use action words and you will start writing achievement statements that are impactful. Show how you produced positive results from the various tasks that you were assigned.

IMPORTANT: Make sure you include in your résumé any statements which demonstrate your abilities in three areas which are common to almost any job role:

1. **Communication** (e.g. written, verbal, presentations, customer service, with different levels of staff, management and customers)

2. **Efficiency** (e.g. less errors, increased customer satisfaction, % more orders, % less server downtime)

3. **Data Management/Technical/Hands-On Skills** (e.g. typing speed, software packages, phone systems, cash registers, etc.)

accelerated	captured	delivered	explored	increased
accomplished	catalogued	demonstrated	expressed	influenced
achieved	centralized	designated	extended	informed
acquired	chaired	designed	extracted	initiated
acted as	charted	detected	fabricated	innovated
active in	checked	determined	facilitated	inspected
adapted	clarified	developed	familiarized	inspired
addressed	classified	devised	filed	installed
adjusted	coached	directed	finalized	instilled
administered	collaborated	discovered	financed	instructed
advanced	collected	dispatched	fixed	insured
advised	combined	dispensed	focused	integrated
advocated	commanded	displayed	followed through	interacted
aided	commended	dissected	followed up	interfaced
allocated	communicated	distributed	forecasted	interpreted
analyzed	compared	documented	forged	interviewed
answered	compiled	drafted	formatted	introduced
applied	completed	earned	formed	invented
appraised	composed	edited	formulated	investigated
approved	computed	educated	fostered	involved
arbitrated	conceived	effected	found	issued
arranged	conceptualized	eliminated	founded	joined
assembled	conducted	emphasized	fulfilled	judged
assessed	conserved	employed	functioned	justified
assigned	consolidated	enabled	gained	launched
assisted	constructed	enacted	gathered	lectured
assured	consulted	encouraged	generalized	led
attained	contacted	enforced	generated	liaised
attended	continued	engineered	governed	lifted
audited	contracted	enhanced	graduated	listened
augmented	contributed	enlarged	granted	lobbied
authored	controlled	enlisted	groomed	located
authorized	converted	ensured	grossed	logged
awarded	conveyed	entertained	grouped	maintained
balanced	convinced	equipped	guided	managed
began	coordinated	established	handled	manufactured
billed	corresponded	estimated	headed	mapped
boosted	counselled	evaluated	helmed	marketed
bought	created	examined	helped	mastered
briefed	critiqued	exceeded	hired	maximized
broadened	culminated in	excelled	hosted	measured
brought about	cultivated	executed	identified	mediated
budgeted	customized	exhibited	illustrated	merged
built	debugged	expanded	implemented	met
calculated	decided	expedited	improved	minimized
campaigned	defined	experimented	improvised	mobilized
canvassed	delegated	explained	incorporated	moderated

modernized	presented	refined	simplified	taught
modified	presided	regulated	simulated	terminated
monitored	prevented	rehabilitated	sold	tested
motivated	printed	related	solicited	tightened
navigated	prioritized	remodelled	solidified	totalled
negotiated	processed	rendered	solved	tracked
netted	procured	reorganized	sorted	traded
nominated	produced	repaired	spearheaded	trained
notified	programmed	replaced	specialized	transcribed
obtained	projected	reported	specified	utilized
offered	promoted	represented	spoke	transferred
opened	proposed	researched	sponsored	transformed
operated	protected	resolved	staffed	translated
optimized	proved	responded	standardized	transmitted
orchestrated	provided	restored	started	treated
ordered	publicized	retrieved	stimulated	troubleshot
organized	published	revamped	studied	tutored
originated	purchased	reviewed	substituted	uncovered
outlined	qualified	revised	succeeded	undertook
overcame	questioned	revitalized	suggested	unified
overhauled	raised	revived	summarized	united
oversaw	ran	routed	supervised	updated
participated	rated	saved	supplemented	upgraded
perceived	reached	scheduled	supplied	used
perfected	realized	screened	supported	validated
performed	received	searched	surpassed	verified
persuaded	recognized	secured	surveyed	visited
piloted	recommended	selected	sustained	vitalized
pinpointed	reconciled	served	synchronized	volunteered
pioneered	recorded	serviced	synthesized	weighted
placed	recruited	set goals	systematized	welcomed
planned	rectified	set up	streamlined	widened
played	reduced	shaped	strengthened	won
predicted	re-evaluated	shifted	structured tabulated	worked
prepared	referred	shipped	targeted	wrote

Make your descriptions consistent and strong. Notice that all of the above action words are the same tense. It is important that your entire experience section be consistent in terms of grammatical tense. Either all the verbs should be in past tense or present tense. Past tense is recommended. As well, each bullet point should start with an action word to maintain the consistency.

Example: Using action words

Original description	New description
Recording WSIB regulated documents	Recorded WSIB regulated documents
Supply chain purchasing and tracking	Conducted supply chain purchasing and tracking
Prepared weekly contractor payroll	Prepared weekly payroll .
Responsible for change requests	Processed change requests.
Answered phones	Acted as liaison between clients and support staff
Wiped tables	Created healthy environment for customers and maintained positive public image.
Served customers at KFC	Served 85 customers an hour and kept wait time down.

Example: Concise statements

BEFORE:	AFTER:
Recruited to manage the women's division and oversee the opening of the Bloor Street Store.	Recruited to manage women's division and oversee Bloor Street store opening.
Promoted within five months to Vice-President and General Manager of the downtown Montreal store.	Promoted within five months to Vice-President and General Manager of downtown Montreal store.
Managed and controlled all aspects of the company's presence on Vancouver Island.	Managed and controlled all aspects of company's Vancouver Island presence.
Coordinated and supervised all aspects of the opening of the Winnipeg Store.	Coordinated and supervised all aspects of Winnipeg store opening.
Facilitated the development of management and staff to ensure store growth and minimize turnover.	Facilitated management and staff development to ensure store growth and minimize turnover.
Created a high profile for the store through effective personal relations with the marketing community, Chamber of Commerce, the Fashion Council of Toronto and charity organizations.	Created high profile for store through effective personal relations with marketing community, Chamber of Commerce, the Fashion Council of Toronto and charity organizations.

✍Exercise: How would you rewrite these statements?

- Worked and led a team of developers.

- Did Help Desk tickets.

- Responsible for typing reports.

- Various admin tasks.

- I enjoy meeting people and fixing there problems.

- Provided correct answers to customers' questions.

- Responsible for production costs.

✍Exercise: Rewriting Your Experience

Review your work experience worksheet from earlier in the chapter. Rewrite as much of the activities as possible to give them greater impact and seem more relevant. Can you add any skills learned if you rewrite them? How can adjectives make them more powerful?

Create a Master Experience section that includes all your experiences and skills regardless of significance. This master will be used as a template for future résumés.

Honours and Activities Section

This section can be used if you don't have a lot of related work experience. By listing any awards, achievements and/or activities, you can highlight key characteristics that would interest an employer such as leadership skills, mentoring, teamwork and ambition to name but a few. Honours and Activities can be as important as the Education and Experience sections.

What is an Honours and Activities section?

This section of the résumé highlights the relevant activities you have been involved with and the honours you have received that you could discuss with your prospective employer. You also want to communicate how these activities and honours might make you an asset to the organization.

An honours and activities section might include the following:

- Academic awards and scholarships.
- Membership in campus, national, or international organizations.
- Leadership positions held in campus, national, or international organizations.
- University and community service positions.
- Work-related awards or honours.
- Date of award or dates of involvement in an activity.

Samples:
- BMO Outstanding Student Scholarship 2007.
- Copy Editor, McGill University's student newspaper August 2005-December 2006.
- Coach, local YMCA soccer team August 2004-December 2005.
- Vice President, Southern Saskatchewan National Honour Society August 2003-May 2004.

Why write an Honours and Activities section?

- To customize your résumé for specific positions.
- To provide evidence of your qualifications.
- To demonstrate that your work has been recognized as of a high quality by others.
- To provide evidence that you are a well-rounded person.
- To stand out and show how unique of an individual you are.
- To reflect your values and commitment.

Where should you place this section?

The Honours and Activities section is generally placed after the education and experience sections of the résumé. Since this section is usually the last one on the résumé, you can include as many or as few honours and activities as space permits.

How to build your honours and activities section

It is best to brainstorm a list of all your honours and activities before you write the honours section of the résumé. Then you can choose the most relevant and recent honours and activities from your list. Remember that this section is supposed to help you stand out from the crowd and demonstrate your qualifications for a position. Consequently, you may not need or want to include all of the honours and activities on the résumé.

Samples:

Scholarships
Millenium Four-Year Academic Scholarship 2006-20010
MBNA Scholarship Award for Student Academic Excellence 2004-2006

Academic Honours
Dean's List 2008-present
Who's Who among Ottawa College and University Students 2008

Leadership Positions
Phi Kappa Delta (International Speech Honour Society) Vice-President 2004-2006
Secretary of Correspondence of York University's Chapter of the Honour Society 2005-2007

Membership in Professional Organizations
Eta Kappa Nu (Electrical Engineering Honour Society) 2004-present
Future Marketers of Canada 2007-2009

University Service Positions
Freshmen Engineering Academic Counseling 2004-2006
Residence Hall Freshmen Council 2006-2008

Community Service Positions
YMCA Cub Scouts Assistant Scoutmaster 2005-present
Vaughan Region Adult Reading Program Tutor 2006-present

Public Service Positions
Humane Society Volunteer, 2007-2009
Hospital for Sick Children Walkathon Fundraiser, 2008

Awards
National Writing Golden Quill Award, 2009
Kiwanis Boys & Girls Volunteer of the Year Award, 2006
Central Tech Student Excellence Award, 2007 & 2008

Let's think…

About you…

- What activities have you been involved with in the past and in the present?

- What kinds of activities and honours are valued most highly in your field?

- Which of your activities and honours are most closely associated with your career goals?

- Which of your activities and honours will the company to which you are applying consider most valuable?

- What does your involvement in activities, related and unrelated to your career goals, reveal about you and your values? How can you "sell" these activities to an employer?

About the company or organization…

- What are the values considered most important by the company you are applying to or by the field in general?

✎ Exercise: List Your Honours and Activities

Complete your honours and relevant activities (including extracurricular activities, awards, grants, prizes and special honours, memberships in professional clubs and organizations and /or volunteer activities).

Title / Position	Sponsors / Affiliated Organizations	Responsibilities or Skills Learned	Dates of Involvement
Class Organizer	Habitat for Humanity Canada	Coordinate schedules Construction Generate volunteers Ongoing communication with volunteers and organizers Track status Report successes	Feb – May 2009
Winner of Teamwork Award	Business for Kids Program	Mentor Grade 5 class Generate brainstorming Secure event booth Secure materials Advise on marketing Communicate to kids Coordinate with teachers, Principal and organizers	Sept 2008 – June 2009
Officer	GCI Student Council	Record meeting minutes Schedule meetings Distribute minutes and status reports Coordinate social events and fundraisers Manage campaign Act as back-up Treasurer	Sept. 2007- June 2009

Styles to choose from: (depending on the amount of available space on your résumé). Ideally, if you have an activity that matches some of the skills your prospective employer is looking for, you would want to use the detailed version. Otherwise, the minimal style should suffice.

Minimal	Detailed
Photography Club, University of Toronto January 2005 – Present	President, Photography Club, University of Toronto, January 2005 – Present Organized campus event Increased membership with promotional efforts

Tailoring For Your Audience

The activities and honours section of the résumé is a great place to tailor the résumé for specific positions, companies, and organizations. This section can become customized for specific positions since you will probably not include all of your activities and honours but only those that make your résumé stronger. To tailor this section for your audience, you should apply the same principles that you used in tailoring the experience section of your résumé.

You should:

Select and include only your most relevant experiences:

Based upon your career goals and the qualifications desired by the company, you will likely find that certain activities and honours are less relevant for specific positions. For example, if you are applying for a video game developer position, your role as a youth leader in a local group may not interest your audience. If you are applying for a teaching position, however, this same activity might be very relevant.

Place your most relevant experiences first:

Since readers are most likely to read information closer to the top of the page, place your most impressive experiences first.

Appeal to your company's values and culture:

If the employer or job description values problem solving or collaborative teamwork, then be sure to include activities and honours from your list that demonstrate that you possess those skills.

Be sure the reader will understand all the acronyms and jargon you use in your résumé.

Résumés in the high-tech field are notorious for these mysterious terms. Imagine a Human Resources Assistant receives a résumé containing the following acronyms and jargon: MCSE, MCP+I, TCP/IP, CCA, CCNA, token ring and PCMCIA network interface cards for LAN connectivity, NT Service Packs, Ethernet cards, Server 4.0, SQL 6.5, 7.0, Red Hat Linux 6.1, Turbo Linux 4.0 and Caldera 2.3, Cisco 2500 routers and switches.

Now, chances are that employers in this jobseeker's field understand all these terms. Just be **sure** that's the case. Spell out any acronyms you think could be questionable, and explain any terms you think some readers of your résumé might not understand.

University / College students, too, need to be aware of "inside" jargon. Like any large organization, whether educational or corporate, acronyms are used frequently. For example, at the University of Toronto, there is a volunteer organization called "ARC" (Academic Retiree Centre); an internship program called "PEY" (Professional Experience Year); and a partnership program called "CCP" (Centre for Community Partnerships). If you participated in activities of those programs, it would be tempting to list the acronym with the assumption that either the reader will understand it or you will have an opportunity to define them in your interview. Don't make those assumptions. If you have acronyms that the reader isn't guaranteed to know, you might as well eliminate that experience.

Look at your résumé from an outsider's perspective and explain (or eliminate) any unfamiliar terms or acronyms.

Here are some more samples of tailored résumés:

Bob Jefferson
122 8th Street, Apt. 312, Kitchener, ON N1N 1N9
(519) 555-9876 † bjeff12@hotmail.com

Objective

To obtain a Corporate Law Assistant position with Minden, Gross LLP to help strengthen the corporate practice area of your firm.

Education
University of Waterloo, Waterloo, ON
Candidate for B.A. degree in English
- Focus: Professional Writing; Pre-Law
- Expected to graduate in May 2010

Work Experience
Fogler Law Group – Corporate Law, *Internship*   02/08 – Present
- Prepare case summaries, file, and perform miscellaneous tasks upon attorney's request.

Doncaster Auto Body, Finance Management Administrator   05/03 – 12/07
- Analyze cash and cheque transactions, supervise customer and employee problems, and operate the central computer system.

Awards/Honours
- The National Dean's List   05/07
- Member of International Honour Society   02/06 – Present
- Active member of Phi Alpha Delta, International Law Society 12/05 – Present

Skills
- Operating Systems: Microsoft Windows XP/2000 and Macintosh OS
- Software: Microsoft Office 2000/2003, Adobe Photoshop 7.0, Pro-Law
- Bilingual in English and French, proficient in Italian
- Punctual, hard working, and dedicated with great initiative and leadership skills

References

Available upon request.

Bobby Singh
400 East Yonge Drive
Fredericton, PEI P0P 0P0
(615) 555-5555
TeenJobSeeker@TeenJobs.com

QUALIFICATION SUMMARY

I am a dependable and highly self-motivated person with excellent customer service and problem solving skills.

EDUCATION

Denlow High School
Fredericton, PEI
Graduated December 2009
GPA 3.45

PROFESSIONAL EXPERIENCE

Library Assistant
City of Fredericton, Fredericton, NB
Responsibilities:

- Assist visitors in the library.
- Keep shelves organized.

ACHIEVEMENTS

Earned the Golden Star employee recognition award three times.

COMPUTER SKILLS

I am highly skilled in Microsoft Office.

PROFESSIONAL MEMBERSHIPS

DECA - National Competitor 2008 – Student Member

AWARDS AND HONORS

2006-2009 Dean's List

ACTIVITIES

2008-Present
       Student Council – Acted as President
       National Honours Society – Acted as IFC Treasurer

Disguising Employment Gaps

What's wrong with a few gaps in your full-time work history? Isn't everyone entitled to a little time off? Many responsible professionals have taken breaks in their careers to travel, take care of ill parents, recover from illness, and a myriad of other legitimate projects.

But for some reason, employers don't like to see gaps in your work history. They would rather see the unemployed time explained, especially if the explanation in any way connects with your job objective, or at least shows strength of character.

A gap in your work history may cause the reader to think, "This person is hiding something" or "Here's someone who might have a problem (such as substance abuse, incarceration, laziness, or instability)". To gain the employer's trust, it's important to justify your employment gaps.

If you have a period of unemployment in your history, here are some ways of dealing with it:

1. Use only years, not months, when referring to spans of time in your work history. This format makes it quicker for the reader to grasp the length of time and can eliminate the need to explain some gaps that occurred within two calendar years.

   Notice the gap in this presentation:
   12/05-3/09 Manager Friendly's Ice Cream Parlour, Vancouver, BC
   2/02-1/04 Manager Lyon's Restaurant, Burnaby, BC

   Without the months, there is no apparent gap:
   2005-2009 Manager Friendly's Ice Cream Parlour, Vancouver, BC
   2002-2004 Manager Lyon's Restaurant, Burnaby, BC

2. If your employment gap between full-time jobs covers two calendar years or more, you may need to explain the gap. Consider all the things you were doing (volunteer work, school activities, internships, schooling and travel) during that time and present them in terms that are relevant to your job objective if possible.

   Someone looking for a medical sales position who took care of an ill parent for two years might say:
   1998-2000 Home Care Provider for terminally ill relative

   An applicant for a travel agent position could refer to their vacation:
   1998-1999 Independent Travel: Europe, Asia, and South America

   A re-entry mother wanting to be a teacher's aide might put:
   1988-1999 Full-time Parent and PTA Volunteer, St. John's Academy

3. If your gap has no apparent relevance to your job objective, explain the gap honestly and with dignity. References to illness, unemployment (even if it is clearly due to a recession)

and rehabilitation, raise red flags in most cases, so avoid those at all cost. Although employers can't discriminate for illness issues, they may see it as a potential risk that you will incur future absences and health benefit costs. Be prepared to speak about something else that you were doing during that time, even if it doesn't relate to your job objective.

Suggested "job titles":

Independent Study
Personal Travel
Adventure Travel
Writing Book
Travels to .....
Home Management
Family Management
Family Financial Management

4. If you use unpaid experience in your work history, be sure that you entitle the section either "Work History" or "History", not "Employment History" or "Professional History", since "employment" and "professional" both imply that you were paid.

Example of Unemployment Gaps

On the next page, this job seeker is currently unemployed and seeking a job in the same field of work that she previously held. Under "Work History", she handled job hopping and employment gaps by listing only years (not months) and she gave the name of the agency where she completed temporary work assignments. She has no Degree but listed relevant training under "Education". You will notice that she used a Functional résumé format.

Wendy Fisher

687 Pape Avenue
Winnipeg, MА B2B 2B3
204-555-6978
Wfisher23@primus.com

Objective:
Administrative position using my strong skills in desktop publishing.

Highlights of Qualifications:

- Experienced office worker and administrator; successful in desktop publishing and systems administration
- Skilled working with:
  - Windows Vista, Windows 2000, Windows NT
  - Microsoft Office
  - Adobe Illustrator and Photoshop
- Energetic self-starter with strong communication skills, works well independently or on a team.
- Highly productive managing projects, a creative problem-solver who rapidly adapts to changing demands.

Professional Experience:
Desktop Publishing & Project Coordination

- Published marketing materials for Extendicare, the nation's largest developer of healthcare facilities.
- Extensively utilized PCs with the latest technologies and programs for JDL and Extendicare.
- Performed marketing research for Extendicare on products, services and companies via the Internet.
- Planned installation of Windows network with ISDN for JDL; oversaw network consultant.

Office Administration & Support:

- Managed office, performing customer service, supervision and accounting for Baxter.
- Experienced working in variety of industries including printing, manufacturing and development.
- Utilized databases and accounting programs to organize and maintain company records.
- Maintained JDL's network of eight computers and three printers.
- Trained personnel on customized software programs.
- Kept Baxter's web press in production 24/7; planned and upgraded printing equipment.

Work History:

2004 to 2009	Administrative Assistant in Marketing	Extendicare, Brandon, MB
2000 to 2004	Office Manager	JDL, Winnipeg, MB
1999 to 2000	Customer Service Temp	Hunt Personnel, Winnipeg, MB
1996 to 1999	Pre-Press Manager	Baxter Inc., Brandon, MB

Education:
University of Manitoba, Winnipeg, MB
>   Visual Design for Computer Professionals, 2004
>   Adobe Illustrator & Adobe Photoshop, 2003

Sherman College, Brandon, MB
>   Business Administration Diploma

✎ Exercise: First Draft

Write the first draft of your own résumé using the exercises above. Create one in a functional format and another in a chronological format to see which suits your experience better.

List all of your experience and education regardless of length to create a master template. Once you see it all listed then you can edit it accordingly. It is ideal that you have one version that lists everything so that you have a template in which to tailor for each job you apply for. You can remove whatever is irrelevant to the position but keep the template for later use as you may want to highlight other experience / education for a different job later.

Here's a functional and chronological worksheet to help you put together the first draft.

Functional Worksheet:

Contact Info:
Objective:
Education:

Work History/Experience:

Honours and Achievements

References: Available upon request.

Chronological Worksheet:

Contact Info:

Objective:

Work History/Experience:

Education

Honours and Achievements

References: Available upon request.

Check: Are you using the best "Action" words?

- ✓ Have you used results? (i.e. served 85 customers per hour, reduced complaints by 15%, increased volume by 72%, closed 230 help desk tickets per week, tracked budget of $100K+).
- ✓ Are all the verbs in past tense?
- ✓ Are you addressing the role / job that you are applying for?
- ✓ Did you use the word "I"? (Don't!)
- ✓ Did you remove irrelevant information?
- ✓ Is the format consistent with font, spacing and centering?
- ✓ Is there enough white space or is it too crammed together?
- ✓ Is the font legible?
- ✓ Are there any pictures or clip art? (Don't!)

Remember to review the final product.

- ✓ **Keep it Simple** – Be clear and concise. Make sure it is easy to read and understand.
- ✓ **Structure** – Use short sentences, bullet points and high impact words. You only have a small amount of words with which to capture your potentials interest. Make them count!
- ✓ **Presentation** – Use standard fonts (Times New Roman or Arial) and line spacing. Keep it traditional. Print on white paper only and make sure you use a quality printer.
- ✓ **Check** – Make sure you check your résumé for spelling mistakes, grammatical errors and sentence structure. These kinds of common mistakes can diminish the effect of your content. Check it over several times then get someone with a fresh perspective to check it as well.
- ✓ **Lies** – Never lie on your résumé. It puts unnecessary pressure on <u>you</u>. Present yourself in a positive way and definitely talk up your attributes. But do not set yourself up to be caught or be put in a situation where you don't know what you're doing.
- ✓ **Accuracy** – Any qualifications, work experience, references or awards should be double checked for accuracy. This is in terms of names, dates and institutes.

Statistics show that approximately one in three people lie on their résumés. Don't be one of those people! If you are ever caught lying during the interview, you will not get the job (or any other job opening that they will have in the future). And, if you get caught after you are hired, you can be fired "on-the-spot" for false misrepresentation. Then try explaining that incident on your résumé for future employment!

Judge a Résumé by its Cover Letter

General Considerations and Tips

A cover letter / email is a necessary business letter that accompanies your résumé whether you mail, email, or fax your application and / or résumé. Its purpose is to introduce your résumé, express your personality and enthusiasm for the position, highlight your key skills that match the job requirements and provide support for your candidacy that is not covered by your résumé. Writing a cover letter / email can be a challenging and time-consuming task, especially when you must customize it towards each organization and position. The following suggestions are offered when writing a cover letter/email.

- You must address the following four questions somewhere in your cover letter/email:
  - ❓ *Why you? (i.e. what makes you a great fit for this job / company?)*
  - ❓ *Why this job? (i.e. why are interested in this job? Focus on the fit, not on your personal career objectives.)*
  - ❓ *Why this company? (i.e. what is it about this company that makes you a good fit?)*
  - ❓ *Why now? (i.e. why are you looking for work? Graduated? Laid off? Ready to progress in your career?)*

- If sending via snail mail, ensure that each letter uses the same font and high quality paper as the résumé.

- If printing, use 1 inch margins all the way around and print on high quality white résumé paper (8" x 11") using a laser or high quality inkjet printer. Don't use flashy coloured paper.

- Proof your letter / email for grammar and spelling errors! Or have someone else proof it for you. There's nothing worse than a spelling mistake or "typo" on a job application!

- Be brief and concise; the cover letter should be approximately 1 page in length.

- Expand on your résumé rather than repeat the résumé's content.

- Individualize and target each cover letter to the position you seek. Remember - you are trying to convince someone why you're the best person for that particular job.

- Be sure to market yourself. Explain what you can offer the company, not what the company can do for you.

- Always include a cover letter with your résumé, whether it is mailed, e-mailed, or faxed!

- If mailed or faxed, remember to sign the cover letter.

- If e-mailing your cover letter, remember to "attach" your résumé and any other documentation as outlined by the employer in their application instructions. If they want your résumé as an ASCII text file (i.e. no stylish formatting - as in MS Word) then send it that way. If you can't follow their instructions, they probably won't hire you.

- Make it Personal. If you are researching cover letters, there are numerous standardized template options. These may be helpful to others but for the young job seeker it is important to address your employers personally. Let them know that you understand the job you are applying for and that you have researched the company.

  Show them that you mean business by highlighting that you have taken the time to make each application specific to the job you're applying for.

- Sell yourself. This is a prime opportunity to distinguish you from the other applicants. Your cover letter should include a few brief, succinct sentences or bullet points on why your skills would meet the needs of the job you are applying for. Speak to the qualifications that they have listed in the job posting, if there is one. Use adjectives and examples to create an impact.

Open The Door With Your Cover Email

Your cover letter or email should explain why you are sending your résumé. Never send a résumé without a covering letter unless you are explicitly asked not to by an employer's application instructions. Do not make the reader guess what you are asking for - be specific! Tell the employer you are writing about the part-time summer elementary opportunity or the permanent position in high school chemistry posted on the Toronto District School Board ("TDSB") website. If you no job posting to refer to, let them know that you are writing because you didn't see any positions in grade 4 physical education on the TDSB website and you would like to know of any upcoming opportunities in school district #45.

Don't forget to:

✓ Always state specifically how you learned about the position or the organization - the Workopolis website, your university academic advisor, your neighbour Mrs. Blake. It is always appropriate to mention the name of someone who suggested that you write.

✓ Remember you are trying to convince the reader to look at your résumé. The cover letter is the first impression - there are no second chances for a first impression! The cover letter must be well written and targeted specifically to the employer you are writing.

✓ Call attention to the highlights of your background -- education, experience, leadership roles -- which are relevant to the position you are applying for. Be specific and use examples.

✓ State exactly what is enclosed or attached - résumé, list of references, transcripts forthcoming etc., so that the employer knows what you included in your application package.

✓ Provide additional information not referred to or requested in the application such as your availability date for an interview and / or start date and when you will follow up via mail / e-mail or telephone.

✓ Show your motivation. Explain why you are pursuing the job and what interests you about the opportunity.

✓ Don't forget to give your key contact details (phone and email).

✓ Always be professional. Don't use funny pictures, street slang, inappropriate references or questionable humour.

For example:

   o "I heard about the class action lawsuit against your company. I won't join it if you give me the job."
   o "I know Suzie Baxter who works in accounting. She is so hot."
   o "I enjoyed the University of Toronto except for morning classes when I had a hangover."

Top Mistakes

Many job seekers spend hours crafting each item on their résumé. Then they whip out a quick cover letter full of errors - not realizing that a cover letter is just as important as a résumé.

One common cover letter goof: typos and spelling errors. In order to avoid these opportunity killers, always spell-check the document. Then read the document out loud - you may catch spelling errors the computer missed (such as accidentally writing "jog" instead of "job" or "hope to hear from you shorty"). Only after you have double-checked your cover letter should you attach it to your résumé and send it off.

Here are some other all-too-common cover letter blunders and how to fix them.

Name That Job

What's one of the first things you should do after writing your greeting to the reader of a cover letter? State exactly which job you're applying for. Include the exact name of the position. If the posting provided a job ID number then include that too. It's also a good idea to mention where you initially heard about the opening.

There's a good reason for being so specific. Many recruiters or HR personnel handle hundreds of job openings, so they won't automatically know which one you're gunning for. By reminding them of the specific opening for which you're applying, you'll make it more likely that your résumé will be read by the right person. Besides, anything you can do to make a recruiter's job easier will put you on their good side.

The Danger of Form Cover Letters

Do you send the exact same cover letter to every employer, only changing the name of the person to whom you're sending it? Big mistake!

The point of a cover letter is to make a personal connection with the reader. So to write a successful cover letter, you should tailor it specifically to each company you send it to. For instance, display knowledge of the company history or write about recent events or projects the company has undertaken. This will show that you have taken the time to research the company before sending in your résumé – as well as prove that you really want the job.

Don't Repeat Yourself

A common trap that many job seekers fall into when writing a cover letter is to simply regurgitate everything that's in their résumé. But if it's already in your résumé, then you're just wasting your breath ... and a chance at the job.

A cover letter should not be a rehash of your résumé; instead, it should offer deeper insights into what your résumé does NOT say. Provide an in-depth explanation of some of your key achievements at your last job for instance and how those accomplishments could help the company. Target a unique qualification from the job posting that you have experience in or tell a brief story about a tough problem you solved. The point is: the reader already has your résumé - the cover letter should add to it, not repeat it.

What Can You Do for Me?

When writing a cover letter, many people discuss why s/he needs the job.

"I need the money."

"I find the position interesting."

"I've wanted to work for you since I was a kid."

"I need more experience in the industry."

"Since your company is the best in the industry, a job there would help my career."

"It has been my lifelong passion to work in the Sports Industry."

Alert!: Companies don't really care about your needs. They're not hiring you to enrich your life or provide you with an income. They're hiring you because they need a job done.

That means your cover letter should focus on the company's needs and how you can fulfill them, not what the company can do for you.

A good way to start: Look at the requirements for the position in the job posting. Then, in your cover letter, discuss point by point how you meet (or even exceed) those requirements. By using the job posting as a guide, you'll show the company how hiring you will benefit them and not just you.

One last note: Try to be both confident and humble when discussing what you can offer the company. While you certainly want to appear competent, arrogance can turn off a hiring manager. Show enthusiasm, confidence and keep a positive attitude and your cover letter will take you far.

Example:

The following is a sample that incorporates all these tips. It should give you a clear idea about what is required for an effective cover letter and it will clarify anything you don't understand.

Example Cover Letter– Teen Jobs

June 26, 2008

Hunter Marketing
659 13th Street
Montreal, QC H3C 3C3

Job Title: Junior Marketing Assistant

Dear Mr Mustafa,

Your position advertised on Monster is an excellent match with my abilities. I am in my final year of high school and have been accepted into WLU next year. I will be majoring Business and Marketing. I would like the opportunity to be considered for the part time junior position you are currently advertising.

I have been interested in Marketing for some time now and am very eager to begin a career in this area. The opportunity to work with seasoned professionals in a junior role is very appealing to me as I am seeking experience and a chance to learn from people in the industry. Hunter is the kind of company I see myself working for in the future.

I have gained experience in Marketing and Advertising through working as part of the marketing team on the student newspaper. I have found this experience to be invaluable as I have been involved in strategic problem solving, communications and implementation of marketing strategies. I have excellent creative writing skills with a particular speciality in high impact targeted writing.

I would like the opportunity to help Hunter Marketing achieve their goals. I feel that my creative writing skills and experience will bring a fresh perspective to Hunter. I am self-motivated, versatile and I am able to provide Hunter with a high output of creativity. The skills I have learnt working on the school newspaper have equipped me to meet specific needs in a high-pressure environment. I can deliver goal-oriented results within tight time constraints and am able to work as part of a multifunctional team. I think these key qualities make me an excellent candidate for this position.

Thank you for taking the time to consider my application. If you require any further information I am available to meet with you personally. I look forward to becoming a valuable team member with your company and I will follow up soon to confirm that my résumé has been received.

You may contact me at 604.555.5555 or via email at ariley0092@primus.com

Best regards,

Alex Riley
Ariley0092@primus.com
604.555.5555 (H)

How do I know what will impress prospective employers?

In order to impress prospective employers when writing a cover letter, you must first know what they are looking for in candidates. Learning more about the company itself—and what they value—can help you do this. Here are some suggestions:

- Read the job posting carefully.

- Research the corporate website, read and try to understand their mission statement. Sometimes an organization's mission may not be clearly stated.

- Network with "insiders" (people that work with the company).

- Refer to your school's career center or search for more information on the internet.

What do I include in my cover letter heading?

The heading provides your contact information, the date you are writing and the address of the company to which you are applying.

For your contact information, you will want to include the following:

- Your name.

- The address where you can be reached. (optional if you're sending it electronically via email, website or fax.)

- Phone number. Ideally, there should be voicemail so that a message can be left when you are not available. The outgoing message to callers must be professional.

- E-mail address. Remember, it must be a professional-type address. Do not use anything too casual like hottie@hotmail.com.

The contact information should match the information and formatting of the contact information on your résumé.

Include the full date (*month, day, year*) on a separate line. Then include the contact information for the person to whom you are writing:

- Name of the specific person.

- Title of that person (if available).

- Full name of the company. For example, use "The Coca-Cola Company Ltd.", not "Coke".

- Address of the company. If no address is available, use the email address or fax number to which you are submitting. (Not necessary if your cover letter is an email unless you are attaching your cover letter to the email as a document.)

Example:

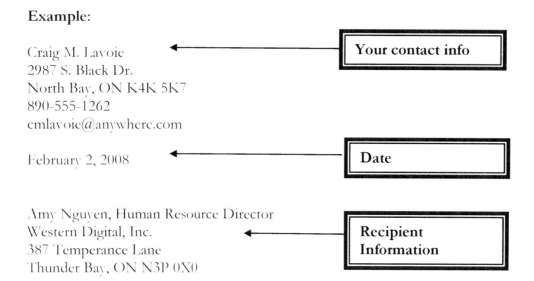

Craig M. Lavoie
2987 S. Black Dr.
North Bay, ON K4K 5K7
890-555-1262
cmlavoie@anywhere.com

February 2, 2008

Amy Nguyen, Human Resource Director
Western Digital, Inc.
387 Temperance Lane
Thunder Bay, ON N3P 0X0

To whom do I address my letter?

Whenever possible, address your letter to a specific individual; usually the person in charge of interviewing and hiring. (Don't assume it is someone in HR.) Doing so will give you a greater chance of having your application packet read and not filed away automatically.

Here are some ideas on how to get the name of a specific person:

- Look in the job posting for the contact person.
- Call the company for more information.
- Research the company's website for the person in charge of the department you are applying to or a person in Human Resources.

If you cannot find the name of that person, you may address your letter to a generic role. For example:

Dear Hiring Professional:
Dear Selection Committee:
Dear Hiring Executive:

If you find the name but cannot decipher the gender of the person, you may address that person using their full name instead of their last name.

What Do I Include In My Introduction?

As the purpose of your introduction is to catch the reader's attention and make you stand out, you need to be as specific as possible in this section. Here are some tips on how to start your introduction and make an immediate connection:

- State the university / college / high school you attend, your major (or applicable courses) and what position you are applying for (if you are a student).
- Mention where you heard about the job.
- Mention the name of a contact that has a positive connection with the company, if any.
- Bring up any previous conversations you have had with your reader (i.e., at a job fair).
- Many people hear of job openings from contacts associated with the company. If you wish to include a contact's name in your cover letter, make certain that your reader has a positive relationship with that person.
- Mention an article, award, speech or association event that the reader has participated in.

In some instances, you may have previously met the reader of your cover letter. In these cases it is acceptable to use your introduction to remind your reader of who you are and briefly discuss a specific topic of your previous conversation(s).

Some examples:

- As a York University junior in the IT Security Management program, I would like to fill the position of Security Analyst Internship advertised on MacAfee's website. Professor Gene Smith speaks highly of MacAfee, and he urged me to write directly to you.
- I have been thinking about our conversation at Concordia's Career Fair on January 26. I agree that a team spirit and strong work ethic are vital for success and I believe I can bring these qualities to your company.

Most importantly, give a brief overview why your values and goals align with the organization's values and how you will be a benefit to them. You should also touch on how you match the position requirements. By reviewing how you align with the organization and how your skills match what they're looking for, you can outline the contents of your cover letter before you write it.

How to make a strong claim for yourself.

After gaining the initial attention of the reader, you must make a strong claim about your candidacy and that you match the needs of the job and the company. State clearly two or three qualifications which you possess that match the company's / position's requirements. These qualifications will then be the focus of your body paragraphs and arguments.

Some examples:

"I agree that a team spirit and strong work ethic are vital for success and I believe I can bring these qualities to your company."

"I believe that my production experience, design skills, and enthusiasm for writing make me a strong candidate for the Production / Design Internship."

What Do I Include In My Body?

Your body content is an important part of your cover letter, because it allows you to persuade your reader why you are a good fit for the company and the job. Carefully choose what to include in your argument. You want your argument to be as powerful as possible but it shouldn't cloud your main points by including excessive or irrelevant details about your past. In addition, refer to your résumé as the source of "data" you will use and expand on in your cover letter.

You need to:

- Show your reader that you possess the most important skills s/he seeks (you're a good match for the organization's mission / goals and job requirements). Look at each requirement. If you feel that you have 70-80% of these skills then highlight the key ones here.

- Convince the reader that the company will benefit from hiring you (how you will help them).

- Include in each paragraph a strong reason why your employer should hire you and how they will benefit from the relationship.

- Maintain an upbeat / personable tone.

- Avoid explaining your entire résumé but use your résumé as a source of information to support your argument (the two documents should work together).

✒ **Reminder**: When writing your cover letter body, it is essential for you to learn as much as possible about the company and the job (see the "*Cover Letter Workshop – Introduction*" resource later in this chapter).

How can I show I am qualified for this position and that I am a good match for the organization?

You don't only want to refer to the skills that you possess; you also need to demonstrate that you possess them! When writing about your skills, you can think of it as telling a story. You should describe the experiences of how you received and grew your skills, mentioning specific places you worked and positions you held.

For example:

"My communication skills in the workplace have grown as a result of my internships. When I was an intern at Smith & Jones, I wrote memos and letters to customers and colleagues on a daily basis. This experience taught me to write professionally and to-the-point."

What have I done that illustrates these qualifications?

Along with explaining your skills, you want to describe how your experience with that skill is unique. Many people may have communication skills, but have you won an award or scholarship for technical writing? Be specific and match this information to your résumé.

Here are some ideas about what might set you apart:
- Special projects.
- Explain course work that gives you a type of professional experience.
- Awards.
- Show that others have recognized the high quality of your work.
- Include only those awards that relate to the position you desire.
- Accomplishments.
- Demonstrate how you improved efficiency/productivity at work or school.
- Include what you did at school that proves your skills.
- Explain how you set a goal and reached it.
- Language fluency.

For example:

"While at the University of Guelph, I participated in a collaborative web-consulting project for a Technical Writing class. With two classmates, I served as a web consultant for a local business, Burney Giftware. In order to make feasible recommendations for revisions, additions and deletions to Burney Giftware's website, we conducted interviews, observed the workplace, researched the existing and target customers and completed multiple web analyses. I am confident that these activities have provided me with the experience that you require in the job description."

What Do I Include In My Closing?

Your closing restates your main points and reveals what you plan to do after your readers have received your résumé and cover letter.

The following are recommended tips for closing your cover letter:

- Close with a strong reminder of why you are a good match for the job position and the organization.

- Restate why you align with the organization's mission / goals.

- Restate why your skills match the position requirements and how your experience will help the organization.

- Request an interview in some way.

- Inform your reader when you will contact them. *(If you are applying to a job posting and it stipulates that only selected applicants will be contacted, then don't include this statement.)*

- Provide contact information. Include your phone number and e-mail address.

- Thank your readers for their consideration.

- Sign your name and print it underneath.

A sample closing:

"I am confident that my coursework and work experience in radio engineering will help your Scarborough division attain its goals. I look forward to meeting with you to discuss the job position further. I will contact you before June 5th to discuss my application. If you wish to contact me, I may be reached at 705.555.6473, or by e-mail at joewillis310@ecco.com. Thank you for your time and consideration."

Although, this closing may seem bold, potential employers will read your documents with more interest if they know you will be calling them in the future. Also, many employment authorities prefer candidates who are willing to take the initiative to follow-up. Additionally, by following up, you are able to inform prospective employers that you're still interested in the position and determine where the company is in the hiring process. When you tell readers you will contact them, it is imperative that you do so. It will not reflect well on you if you forget to call a potential employer when you said you would. It's best to demonstrate your punctuality and interest in the company by calling when you say you will.

If you do not feel comfortable informing your readers when you will contact them, ask your readers to contact you, and thank them for their time. For example:

"Please contact me at 705.555.6473, or by e-mail at joewillis310@ecco.com. I look forward to speaking with you. Thank you for your time and consideration."

Another example:

"I am eager to speak with you and discuss my possible contribution to Dream Country Mattress, as I feel my experiences in communication and customer service will be an asset to the company. I will be in touch with you within a week and if you need to reach me, you can call 403.555.1143 or email me at marcus8887@anyplace.com. Thank you for your time and consideration."

If you do not feel comfortable informing your readers when you will contact them, you may simply delete that part of the closing. For example:

"I am eager to speak with you and discuss my possible contribution to Vaughan Press as I feel my experiences in communication and customer service will be an asset to the company. Please contact me at 416.512.1143 or email me at marcus8887@anyplace.com. Thank you for your time and consideration."

Remember: If you say you will call, do not forget to do so.

Formatting and Organization

The cover letter / email is one of the most challenging documents you may ever write: you must write confidently about yourself without sounding arrogant and self-absorbed. The solution to this is to explain how your values and goals align with the prospective organizations and to discuss how your experience will fulfill the job requirements. Before we get to content, however, you need to know how to format your cover letter / email in a professional manner.

Formatting your cover letter

Whether you are printing your cover letter or attaching it to an email in a separate document, it must convey a professional message. Of course the particular expectations of a professional format depend on the organization you are looking to join. For example, an accounting position at a legal firm will require a more traditional format. A position as an Animator at Disney might require a completely different approach. Again, a simple analysis of the company and the position will yield important information about the document format expectations. Let the organization's communications guide your work.

For this example, we are using a traditional approach to cover letters / emails:

- Single-space your cover letter.
- Leave a space between each paragraph.
- Leave three spaces between your salutation (such as "Sincerely" or "Regards") and your name.
- Leave a space between your heading (contact information) and greeting (such as, "Dear Mr. Roberts").
- Either align all paragraphs to the left of the page or indent the first line of each paragraph to the right.
- Use standard margins for your cover letter, such as one-inch margins on all sides of the document.

- Center your letter in the middle of the page. In other words, make sure that the space at the top and bottom of the page is the same.

- If printing, sign your name in black or blue ink between your salutation and typed name.

Before you send the cover letter / email

Always proofread your cover letter / email carefully because once it is sent, there is no way to get it back. After you've finished, put it aside for a couple of days if time allows, then reread it. More than likely, you will discover sentences that could be improved or grammatical errors that could otherwise prove to be uncharacteristic of your writing abilities.

Furthermore, we recommend giving your cover letter to friends and colleagues. Ask them for ways to improve it. Listen to their suggestions and revise your document as you see fit.

Sample:

Ellen Simpson
315-3902 Bloor Avenue West * Ottawa, ON K2L 1K1
Telephone: (613) 555-9900 * elsimps@bucket.com

October 19, 2009

Bob Smith
Manager
International Business Machines
3450 Pharmacy Road
Nepean, ON K1A 2K2

Dear Mr. Smith,

Having achieved many goals in my career as a Bookkeeper and Financial Services Assistant, I am interested in expanding my professional horizons by seeking new challenges in the area of office management. I am interested in a position with your firm and have enclosed my résumé for your review and consideration.

As you can see, my career in business, finance and bookkeeping is extensive. I have enjoyed a reputation as an efficient bookkeeper and have a knack for immediately establishing a good rapport with clients.

As a team member of your organization, I can provide:

- Efficiency, reliability, accuracy with numbers.
- Maturity, honesty, ability to look at challenges as opportunities.
- Knowledge of general and legal office procedures.
- Ability to develop and lead a team.

Mr. Smith, my objective is to establish a time when we can meet to discuss how my talent, professionalism, and enthusiasm will add value to your operation. Thank you for your consideration.

I look forward to speaking with you soon.

Sincerely,

Ellen Simpson

Encl.

Exercise: Good Cover Letter or Bad?

Review the following cover letters and determine whether it is a good cover letter or bad and why?

Cover Letter #1

Michael Maxxim
1000 University Terrace
Apt #100
Regina, SK C7C 4C5

11/2/2009

Kristel Dixon
Director, Human Resources
Joe Fresh Inc.
1020 Hull Street
Hull, QC H3H 6H4
1.888.4.FRESH

Dear Ms. Dixon:

I am a junior at Carleton university, working toward my bachelor's degree in Marketing. I discovered your internship program while researching opportunities in the field of business and marketing. I am writing to inquire about potential positions with Joe Fresh.

My courses in marketing have convinced me that sales and marketing is a career option I would like to explore. More importantly, an internship with Joe Fresh would be mutually beneficial and i would like it very much. Your company has an excellent reputation for customer satisfaction.

I know that the combination of my education and motivation to excel will make me an asset to your marketing department. My enclosed résumé provides additional details about my background.

If possible, I would like to call you next week as to follow up to see if you would review my qualifications and consider me for a position for your company. If so, I hope to schedule an interview at a convenient time. I look forward to speaking with you. Should you have any questions before that time, you may reach me via phone (416.332.5188) or via email jb007@students.carleton.edu).

Thank you for your consideration.

Sincerely,

Name

Cover Letter #1 is NOT a good Cover Letter because:

☒ There is very little substance in their second and third paragraphs.

☒ The "U" in University in the first paragraph is not capitalized.

☒ The I in the second paragraph is not capitalized.

☒ Paragraph 3 has only 2 sentences and does not highlight anything from her résumé.

☒ Lacks emotion.

☒ Asks permission "If possible, I would like to call..." rather than "I will call you....".

Cover Letter #2

1000 Hazel Lane
Truro, NS D4R 4D4
423-555-0900

29 October 2009

Inside Lacrosse
Townline, NB

Dear Inside Lacrosse Magazine,

My knowledge of lacrosse through living it and breathing it growing up, and my avid writing skills are what would make me an asset to the Inside Lacrosse staff. I am now seeking the position of assistant editor that I read about one www.journalismjobs.com.

The experience that I have lies in my internship at Women Supporting Women, which is the local breast cancer support group for the Eastern Shore of Maryland. I currently have three articles published in a local magazine and many more to come. My job before I graduate is to interview local survivors and write their stories to be published once a month for the next year. This internship has helped me to develop an appreciation of deadlines and has helped me strengthen my writing and editing skills.

Lacrosse was a love of mine at one time and to rekindle that with my new love for writing would be magic. I am also very familiar with the Towson area and the local lacrosse scne.

I hope to meet you soon to further discuss the arts reporter position. Please feel free to call me anytime on my cell phone at 413-555-0660 or email me at kb00990@students.carleton.edu.

Sincerely,

Karl Bunson

Cover Letter #2 is a bad Cover Letter

- ☒ There are indents for paragraphs. This should be a block format.
- ☒ There is not a double space between paragraphs.
- ☒ The A and E in Assistant Editor in the first paragraph are not capitalized.
- ☒ The sentence in paragraph 1 that states "I am now seeking the position of assistant editor that I read about one www.journalismjobs.com" needs the word "one" changed to "on." Spelling error.
- ☒ The contact below the date is lacking a person's name and address.
- ☒ The salutation should be to a person not to a magazine.
- ☒ The 3rd paragraph is two sentences and says very little. There is also a spelling error in the last sentence of this paragraph -"scne" should be "scene".

Cover Letter #3

100 Axeton Ct.
Berlin, NL F4F 5G6
(920)555-0007

April 27, 2009

Mr. Adam Crowley
KPMG, Inc.
111 South Calvert Street
St. John's, NL D1D 1D1

Dear Mr. Crowley:

Currently I am a junior in The Rotman Business School at University of Toronto and am actively seeking an internship with a reputable company such as KPMG. I was extremely impressed with KPMG's approach to auditing after attending the presentation given by your firm on April 19, 2007 at Simon Fraser University. After discussing the summer internship program with Keith Meldrum, an SFU student who interned at KPMG, I became even more excited about your internship program . In addition, I talked to other students who interred at KPMG and after I conducted research of my own I confirmed my interest in KPMG. After careful review of my credentials, you will understand why my skills and qualifications are a great match for your intern program.

Upon graduation from The Rotman School of Business with a degree in Accounting in May, 2010, I will complete an internship in the Silver & Co., CPA Firm which lasted for 10 months. This internship provided me with solid analytical and problem solving skills through my responsibility of identifying and resolving financial reporting issues. In addition I learned how to use multiple accounting software applications and acquired skills based on incentive calculations and payments. Account reconciliations and analysis are procedures I was able to master and I participated in preparation and review of consolidated financial statements schedules, research, and journal entries. You will find that I am interested in all facets of accounting, but most of all I am interested in international tax accounting because I have vast multicultural experience and foreign language skills.

I am excited about gathering "real" world experience with such a prestigious firm as KPMG. Being an international student, I possess a diverse, multicultural perspective which I feel is critical to succeed in today's market place. My business overview is truly global by nature and the chance to enhance that overview with KPMG is desirable to say the least. Learning from a firm such as yours will give me a true vision as to what is expected from a university graduate in the world of accounting. If I am selected, I will work extremely hard to learn as much as I can while fully understanding as a college student I do have so much to learn.

Please find my résumé enclosed for your review. I welcome the opportunity to meet with you and would greatly appreciate having the chance to further discuss my skills and qualifications. Thank you for your time and consideration. I look forward to hearing from you soon.

Sincerely,
Jason Browley

Cover Letter #3 is a good Cover Letter

☑ The block format is correct.

☑ The middle two paragraphs highlight accomplishments.

☑ Enthusiasm and emotion is displayed by using words and phrases like "extremely impressed, even more excited, such a prestigious firm, etc.".

☑ All sentences are well written and not too many begin with "I".

☑ This letter truly says this student wants to work for this employer.

☑ No spelling errors.

Cover Letter #4

200 Xavier St. W
Foxboro, AB, 20000
403-555-0000

February 3, 2008

Mr. Alex Smith
University of Calgary
1420 N. Charles St.
Calgary, AB B3B 4B4

Dear Mr. Smith:

I would like to express my sincere interest for a position as an Admissions Counsellor with the University of Calgary. The chance to work for such a reputable institution is without compare and I am excited about this possibility. Every effort will be made to have an impact and contribute in any manner requested.

The knowledge that I have gained through my educational studies provides, what I believe to be, the background necessary to be an effective Admissions Counsellor for the University of Calgary. The courses I have taken required me to become acquainted in a number of diverse areas. With classes such as Developmental Psychology, Human Behaviour, Social Problems, Psychology of Personality, and Infancy and Childhood, I have been able to learn and respond to different situations as required by today's challenging society. As a Resident Assistant I've been able to apply the knowledge that I have learned from these classes with everyday interactions with my residents. For two years I have advised and counselled residents in making career / life decisions. As a Student Admissions Guide, I communicated with the students as well as their families in promoting the University. In addition, I needed to acquire an in-depth knowledge of the University to address the many questions presented to me.

I have been quite active in campus activities, many of which have been instrumental in changes in the campus community. As president of the Union of Indo-Canadian Students, a member of the Resident Assistance Counsel, and the ICCC, I have honed my leadership and public speaking skills. One change included making student organizations more aware of the community issues and how to have an impact within the community.

In conclusion, I would like to again express my enthusiasm and sincere wish to pursue a career with University of Calgary. The opportunity to apply my educational experience and energy with your institution is exciting to say the least. I am confident that I will be a valued asset to the University. Thank you for taking the time to read my letter and I hope to hear from you soon.

Sincerely,

Sandeep Luthra

Cover Letter #4 is a good Cover Letter

☑ The block format is correct.

☑ Strong closing paragraph.

☑ Letter addresses skills required for the job in the middle two paragraphs.

☑ Addressed letter to the person involved in the job search.

☑ Speaks highly of the employer.

☑ Consistent, logical flow to the letter.

☑ No spelling, grammar errors.

⚐ **Tip:**

If a job description is lengthy with a lot of requirements, then break it down into bulleted points. For example,

JOB POSTING:

BOX OFFICE MANAGER. Conduct, oversee subscription and ticket sales for events. Generate and maintain reports, perform accounting activities related to box office revenue, oversee operations. Requires customer service skills and accounting experience.

Bulleted version:

Box Office Manager Requirements:
- Conduct, oversee subscription and ticket sales for events.
- Generate and maintain reports, perform accounting activities.
- Customer service skills and accounting experience.

List your related experience:

My Skills and Experience:
- Box office management including ticketing, maintenance of records and ticket database management.
- Maintain and generate reports.
- Box office accounting transaction and reporting.
- Customer service, seating, and ticketing patrons.

Then you can write an effective letter using by matching the requirements with your skills.

✎ Exercise: Write A Cover Letter

Here is a sample job posting for a receptionist:

Position: Receptionist/Administrative Assistant
Site: Princess Margaret Hospital
Department: Medical Imaging
Scale/Grade: A004
Hours: <u>Days – Weekdays and/or Weekends</u>, and may involve other shifts up to 24 hours per week.
Status: PFT (Permanent Full time)

The RECEPTIONIST/ADMINISTRATIVE ASSISTANT performs a limited number of routine and repetitive activities and functions including: performing reception functions, including: answering, screening and directing telephone calls; scheduling appointments, tests and visits; maintaining schedules for assigned personnel; performing clerical support functions including: word-processing/typing routine correspondence, etc., photocopying; sorting and distributing mail, etc.; providing FAX services; performing cross-functional responsibilities and vacation relief, as required; performing other duties consistent with the job classification.

QUALIFICATIONS

- Completion of Grade XII or recognized equivalent.
- MINIMUM two (2) year related experience.
- Previous on-the-job word-processing experience an asset and Internet competency.
- Experience in health care setting an asset.
- Experience in a customer service field required.
- Excellent organizational skills and telephone etiquette.
- Excellent verbal and written communication skills.
- Position requires the ability to provide important procedure information/preparation, and complicated booking knowledge.
- Good organizational and time management skills.
- Ability to use good judgment in assessing difficult situations.
- Ability to work independently and interdependently as a member of a Health care Team.
- Ability to work with attention to detail and accuracy.
- Knowledge of general office practices, procedures and standards.
- Bilingualism an asset.

POSTED DATE: June 09, 2009

If you are interested in this **full time** position, please quote vacancy **#605192** when applying.

Here is a sample résumé:

Claire Fowles
1234 Cobblestone Drive
Toronto, Ontario M1M 1M1
Home: 647.555.5555
Cell: 647.555.5556
Email: C_Fowles@rogers.com

Objective: Seeking a medical receptionist position that utilizes my extensive computer and medical knowledge, strong organizational abilities, demonstrating quality communications skills and client/patient service.

Qualification Summary: More than 5 years experience as a receptionist in a healthcare setting. Warm outgoing personality. Able to interact effectively and in a supportive manner with persons of all ages and backgrounds. Very good telephone skills and etiquette. Strong ability to work well under pressure and to work accurately and efficiently. Possessor or extensive computer knowledge, Microsoft Excel, and Word, 35 WPM. Bilingual English and French. Knowledgeable of patient billing procedures.

Education: Central Technical High School Toronto, ON
Diploma- 2000
Medical Assistant Certificate

Work Experience: Medical Receptionist, Family Health Clinic, Toronto, ON
Dec. 2003 - present

Greeted patients and agency visitors; directed all people to the appropriate location and services; was courteous, polite and helpful to the public and clients at all times when representing the hospital. Respected and maintained privacy and dignity of agency clients; assured client confidentiality at all times. Provided efficient and professional telephone services; transferred calls according to established protocols. Other duties implied: registering patients according to agency protocols, determining the financial status of patients and their eligibility for the hospital services, assisting patients in accurately completing appropriate forms, and document all information according to hospital protocols.

Medical Receptionist, Axis Community Health Clinic, Concord, ON
Jan. 2000 - Nov. 2003

Scheduled appointments for patients according to established procedures. Collected and posted fees according to protocols; prepared and balanced daily financial registers and submitted all forms and fees to the fiscal department.

Maintained and reported statistics as required. Maintained forms and office supplies required for front desk activities. Secured the building at the close of each working day; turned off or unplugged appliances and machines according to agency protocols and locked all entrances. Daily responsibilities included assuring the readiness of the reception area, opening the building at the designated time and having all front desk activities fully operational at the start of business hours.

References: Available upon request

Write an effective cover letter using the résumé and job posting above. A basic sample is on the next page. Check it after you have completed your exercise.

Claire Fowles
1234 Cobblestone Drive
Toronto, Ontario M1M 1M1
Home: 647-555-5555
Date: 1st May, 2009

Hiring Executive
Princess Margaret Hospital,
610 University Avenue,
Toronto, ON M5G 2M2

Dear Hiring Executive,

I am very interested in joining an organization such as Princess Margaret Hospital. During my research, I was excited to learn about the current opening for a Receptionist/Administrative Assistant (Vacancy #605192), and feel my qualifications and your requirements are a good match. For your review, I have attached my résumé for your consideration.

I have been seeking to transfer my diverse experience working within a busy medical clinic and diploma in Medical Assistance to a hospital environment. Based on the outstanding reputation of Princess Margaret Hospital as a world leader in cancer research, I am confident that the quality of my patient relations and administrative support will match your high standards.

My strong patient care experience, along with my extensive office administration experience would be an immediate asset to your Health Care team. I am highly competent in the areas of patient and physician relations, appointment scheduling, and confidential patient filing and recordkeeping.

Combined with my ability to operate a busy phone service and to communicate fluently in French, I am confident that I would be a good fit for this role.

I would appreciate the opportunity to discuss how my education and experience will be helpful to you. I will be contacting you tomorrow morning on phone to talk about the possibility of arranging an interview.

Thank you in advance for your time and consideration. I look forward to hearing from you soon.

Sincerely,

Claire Fowles
Enclosures:

Cover Letter - Response to an Ad

June 12, 2007

Ms. Holly Peters
Manager
Cool Threads Clothing Store
25 Main St.
Cooksville, Ontario
A1B 2C3

Re: APPLICATION FOR SALESPERSON

Dear Ms. Peters:

I am interested in applying for the position of salesperson at the Hot Threads Store, which was advertised in the June 10 edition of the Cookstown News.

As a high school student, I have developed organizational and communication skills through my involvement in school sports and by coaching junior soccer. I also understand how business operates through my specialization in economics and accounting. I have enclosed my résumé with further details.

I would enjoy being a part of your company and am available for an interview at your convenience. You can contact me at 705.555.1212 or leave a message at 705.555.1234. I look forward to hearing from you.

Sincerely,

Jane Morriseau
78-A Pine Street East
Cooksville, Ontario
P7A 5X3
janeqm@school.ca

Enclosure

Cover Letter - Follows up on a call to an employer

June 12, 2007

Ben Harmon
123 Front Street
Halifax, Nova Scotia
B3K 2X4

Mr. William Jones
Chief Executive Officer
Hightech Inc.
460 Crough Way N.E.
Halifax, Nova Scotia
B3T 4R7

Dear Mr. Jones:

Re: FOLLOW-UP OF EMPLOYMENT WITHIN HIGHTECH INC.

It was a pleasure speaking with you on the telephone last week. Thank you again for taking the time to answer my questions about employment opportunities within your firm.

As you requested, I am forwarding a copy of my résumé. I feel I have many skills which could be used by your organization. I am a resourceful individual who enjoys creative problem solving. I believe my experience at Mine Resources would make me a valuable contributing team member at Hightech Inc.

I am available at your convenience to meet with you to discuss where my skills would benefit Hightech Inc. most. I look forward to hearing from you. You may leave a message at 709.556.7890 in the mornings or call me between 1:30 and 7:00 pm.

Yours truly,

Ben Harmon

Enclosure

Cover Letter - An unadvertised job

James O'Connell
4321 Eatons Way
Calgary, AB T1O O1T

March 1, 2007

Ms. Candace Hamm
Sales Manager
Irwin Food Processing
123 Mason Avenue N.E., Suite 34
Calgary, AB T2A 2A2

Dear Ms. Hamm:

Re : EMPLOYMENT WITHIN IRWIN FOODS

I am a recent graduate of Alpha Beta High School. While I was doing career research on companies that offer in-house training, I noticed that Irwin Foods offers basic courses in marketing and promotions, a field that I am very interested in.

I would appreciate meeting with you to discuss your firm's potential employment opportunities. My Co-op work experience that involved special product promotions may be of interest to you. I have enclosed my résumé with further details.

I will call your Administrative Assistant on March 8, 2007 to see if a convenient appointment time can be arranged. I can also be reached at 403.555.1234 if you prefer to contact me before then.

Yours truly,

James O'Connell
Enclosure

Applying For A Job

There are many things about application letters which can be a "turn-off' for an employer, apart from the NUMBER of applications they may receive, and the fact that so many of these are almost identical.

✍ Exercise: Features... Good or Bad?

Check out these "features" of cover letters listed below...

If you were the person in charge of hiring and saw them in an cover letter, would you classify them as being: very good, O.K., or bad? Why?

Feature	Classification		
1. Prints name at top of letter.	very good	O.K.	bad
2. Addressed letter/email as told to in posting.	very good	O.K.	bad
3. Letter/email is addressed to Personal Officer.	very good	O.K.	bad
4. Employer's name is spelt incorrectly.	very good	O.K.	bad
5. Uses "Dear Sir/Madam" when employer's name is known.	very good	O.K.	bad
6. Uses "To whom it may concern" when name or sex is unknown.	very good	O.K.	bad
7. Does not quote such things as "Position Number" if told to.	very good	O.K.	bad
8. First paragraph states what the letter is about and why you are contacting the recipient.	very good	O.K.	bad
9. Gives no reason why you would like the job.	very good	O.K.	bad
10. Gives a reason why you would like to work for that company.	very good	O.K.	bad
11. Mentions that their résumé, references, etc., are attached.	very good	O.K.	bad
12. Does not include things as asked to by posting.	very good	O.K.	bad
13. Mentions specific times and dates when available for interview.	very good	O.K.	bad

14. Closing paragraph doesn't "encourage" the reader into follow-up.	very good	O.K.	bad
15. Last sentence says "Thank you for your time."	very good	O.K.	bad
16. Last sentence says "Trusting you will give my application some thought.	very good	O.K.	bad
17. Signs "Yours in anticipation."	very good	O.K.	bad
18. Letter/email uses some of the language used in the posting.	very good	O.K.	bad
19. Use of poorly constructed sentences which the reader finds hard to understand.	very good	O.K.	bad
20. Not using Capital Letters in Correct Places.	very good	O.K.	bad
21. Letter is two pages long. (In case of cover email, you have to keep scrolling to get to the end.)	very good	O.K.	bad
22. Bulk of letter/email is written as one complete paragraph.	very good	O.K.	bad
23. Letter is handwritten or email uses non-standard font.	very good	O.K.	bad
24. Uses fancy, coloured or ruled stationery, or uses paper with pre-punched holes or ruled margins.	very good	O.K.	bad
25. Allows one (small) spelling mistake to stay in final letter.	very good	O.K.	bad
26. Reference attached has spelling mistakes.	very good	O.K.	bad
27. Sends in original copies of references, reports, etc.	very good	O.K.	bad
28. Attaches blurred/messy copies of résumé, reference, etc.	very good	O.K.	bad
29. Layout of résumé shows little thought and originality.	very good	O.K.	bad
30. Use of multi-colours in résumé for headings, underlining, etc.	very good	O.K.	bad
31. Encloses copy of résumé even though ad didn't ask for it.	very good	O.K.	bad
32. Pages do not have footers with your name and page numbers on them.	very good	O.K.	bad
33. Letter/email arrives on due date.	very good	O.K.	bad

So, what did you think about these things that may (or may not) appear in application letters? Here are some thoughts, comments, observations, suggestions etc.

Feature	Comments
1. Prints name at top of letter.	Even if you create stationery where your contact information is at the top, your name goes under your signature and contact information should also go at the bottom of the letter/email.
2. Addressed letter/email as told to in posting.	Very Good - that is one of the little "tricks" they are testing for... to see if you can do what you've been instructed to do!
3. Letter is addressed to Personal Officer.	Wrong! The word is Personnel. Only address it to the person and position stated in the ad.
4. Employer's name is spelt incorrectly.	Bad. You just eliminated yourself from getting an interview.
5. Uses "Dear Sir/Madam" when employer's name is known.	How do you expect to make a connection?
6. Uses "To whom it may concern" when name or sex is unknown.	It would be better to use "Dear Sir or Madam" or even phone the company and find out who is to receive the letter. Make sure to get the correct spelling of their name and title. If they refuse to provide that information then use "Dear Hiring Executive".
7. Does not quote such things as "Position Number" if told to.	Always ensure that you include all the details that the ad requests.
8. First paragraph states what the letter is about and why you are contacting the recipient.	Very good. This is what the first paragraph is for...to state that this is an application for position X.
9. Gives no reason why you would like the job.	Don't you want them to know you want the job?
10. Gives a reason why you would like to work for that company.	Only if you've researched the company (which you should) and know what you are talking about. Otherwise, it will sound like a kiss-up.
11. Mentions that your résumé, references, etc., are attached.	Very good. Standard business etiquette.
12. Does not include things as asked to by posting.	Bad! It shows you don't pay attention to detail.
13. Mentions specific times and dates when you are available for interview.	Too pushy. "I'd like to discuss this with you next Monday at 9:37am" is not showing consideration for their schedule or timelines.
14. Closing paragraph doesn't "encourage" the	The last paragraph is to close the deal. You need to show that you are eager to move forward

reader into follow-up.	without being too pushy.
15. Last sentence says "Thank you for your time."	You only thank them for their time when they have spent time with you. Thank them for their consideration.
16. Last sentence says "Trusting you will give my application some thought."	Just by reading it, they are giving their thought. Sounds weak.
17. Signs "Yours in anticipation."	Too desperate.
18. Letter/email uses some of the language used in the posting.	It is always a good idea to try to build your letter/email using some of the language that the employer has used in the ad. It shows that you have, at least, read the ad and perhaps that you know a little bit about what they are talking about. It also makes it easier for them to read because they can see in your letter/email the things they are looking for.
19. Use of poorly constructed sentences which the reader finds hard to understand.	Clearly, not a good idea unless you are Yoda.
20. Not using Capital Letters in Correct Places.	That is Never a Good Idea, is IT?
21. Letter is two pages long. (In case of cover email, you have to keep scrolling to get to the end.)	Not recommended. This is a bit too long especially if it is crammed with text.
22. Bulk of letter/email is written as one complete paragraph.	Back to English class! No breaks between sections make it difficult to read.
23. Letter is handwritten or email uses non-standard font.	Unless you are applying to be a calligrapher, don't ever handwrite a cover letter. And do not use "funny" or overly fancy fonts for your email. You want to express yourself in a professional way.
24. Uses fancy, coloured or ruled stationery, or uses paper with pre-punched holes or ruled margins.	Very bad! If you bring such a résumé into your interview, you will lose your audience. Using this type of paper shows immaturity or a lack of professionalism.
25. Allows one (small) spelling mistake to stay in final letter.	Not fatal, but there is a high risk of being eliminated if there is competition for the job.
26. Reference attached has spelling mistakes.	Serious doubts on the credibility of your referee.
27. Sends in original copies of references, reports, etc.	Never give up originals because you will never see them again. If they wish to see originals in an interview setting, bring them but request that they can take a copy for their files.
28. Attaches blurred/messy copies of résumé, reference, etc.	You are not making a very good impression. Review your electronic copies for format and legibility. Also, make sure that if you are providing documents via email that you are using

	software that the company can open. Most ads will mention acceptable software and version.
29. Layout of résumé shows little thought and organization.	Remember, employers see 1000's of résumés and almost all of them look identical. If you want yours to stand out, you will need to put a lot of thought and originality to survive the screening process. You have 30 seconds to grab their attention.
30. Use of multi-colours in résumé for headings, underlining, etc.	No! Not even for graphic design jobs. If you want to show creativity when applying for creative positions, then include copies of items in your portfolio only if requested. Remember, these are business documents.
31. Encloses copy of résumé even though ad didn't ask for it.	Absolutely essential that you include your résumé even if the ad did not specify for you to include it.
32. Pages do not have footers with your name and page numbers on them.	Do you want to risk losing the first page of your résumé when they print a batch of résumés off at once? Of course not so make sure your name and page number is on all pages after your first page.
33. Letter/email arrives on due date.	Arriving on the due date can suggest that it was a rush job and maybe that is the way you work all the time. If it sits on someone's desk for a few days, they may think you sent it in late and disqualify you.

If you study the following examples you should get a better idea of what a good application letter should look like. Maybe you can even try to write your own application for each advertisement.

EXAMPLE # 1

BROWN'S AIR SYSTEMS APPRENTICE SHEET METAL

We have a vacancy for a person who is interested in a sheet metal apprenticeship. The School Certificate is essential with good results in Technical Drawing, and at least Grade 3 in Mathematics. Interested persons should telephone the Personnel Department for more information at 705.555. 4123 ext 28, and written applications should be addressed to:

Mr. J. Tompkins
Personnel Manager
Brown's Air Systems
P.O. Box 711,
Thunder Bay, ON N1N 1N1

---

20 Bridge Road
Thunder Bay, ON

January 24, 2006

Mr. J. Tompkins,
Personnel Manager,
Brown's Air Systems,
P.0. Box 711,
Thunder Bay, ON N1N 1N1

Dear Mr. Tompkins,

I would like to be considered for the position of apprentice sheet metal worker advertised in the 'Weekly Post' on the 23rd January, 2006.

I have attached my personal résumé, which outlines details of my education, experience and personal information.

For the past three years I attended Technics as an elective at school, and I found the metal work and the drawing very interesting. I became even more interested in sheet metal work after reading about the work and visiting some local factories with the school. After having two weeks work experience with G .B. Melon P/L (Sheet Metal Division), I am now sure that sheet metal work would be the job I'd like.

I will be available to come in for an interview at any time convenient to you. I can be contacted at home on 705.555.6618.

Yours truly,

Omar Athari

EXAMPLE # 2

WANTED - JUNIOR CLERK

Entry level. This position includes a little typing, filing and bookkeeping. It would be suitable for a young person who is interested in office work. Sat. morning work involved. References required.
Apply in writing to:
Tailormade Kitchens
64 Norton Street
Hamilton, ON N1N 1N1

68 Smythe Street,
Hamilton, ON N1N 1N1

February 7, 2006.

The Personnel Manager,
Tailormade Kitchens,
64 Norton Street,
Hamilton, ON N1N 1N1.

Dear Sir/Madam,

I would like to apply for the position of junior clerk which was advertised in the 'Weekly Post' on the 7th February, 2006.

Attached to this letter is a summary of my education, experience and personal information, and copies of my references.

Following a work experience program in September last year, I have become very interested in clerical work. I worked at Patcher Furniture for two weeks so I am familiar with the type of work done in the office of a furniture manufacturer. I learnt filing, invoicing and my typing lessons at Billabong Technical College were also very useful to me during my work experience.

Since then, I have read further on office work, and have talked to several secretaries and clerks. I am sure that clerical work would be a good career for me.

If you wish to interview me, could you please call 519.555.1356 during the day to leave a message? I am available for an interview at any time convenient to you.

Yours faithfully,

Lee Smythe

The Screening Process

"I've missed more than 9000 shots in my career. I've lost almost 300 games. 26 times, I've been trusted to take the game winning shot and missed. I've failed over and over and over again in my life. And that is why I succeed."
— Michael Jordan

The job application process is really a screening process. The slightest mistake in your application give the employer reason to "screen" you out, especially with jobs that have a large number of applicants.

Time is the enemy and the employer will use techniques to save themselves as much time as possible when initially reviewing the pile of applications received. It's often a three step process...

1. Screen applications with obvious errors and poor presentation - employers will most likely give a maximum of 30 seconds to each application at this stage.

2. Of the applications that remain, screen out those that don't address essential criteria, or make it hard to determine whether they do actually have the qualifications / experience requested - will give up to one minute (and not much more) for each application to determine this.

3. The final round will involve a detailed reading of all aspects of the remaining applications in order to determine which of these "most suitable" applicants should be invited in for an interview.

Round One Screening

If there were 100 applications for one position, at least 50% - 70% would be a good number to get rid of in the first round, and if you give them ANY excuse, you will get screened!

The obvious things that will get you screened out immediately include:

- Spelling mistakes.
- Getting their name wrong.
- Not following any instructions stated in the advertisement/job description.
- Not getting application in on time.
- Non professional looking application.

So many people overlook the obvious and that is their undoing!

So... once you've looked after all the "common sense" stuff, you should be more than half way there...

Round Two...

Of the remaining 30-50% of applications, employers would want to eliminate at least half of them in this round. The big question now is how do you make your application stand out from the other applications that survived the first screening?

This is the real question you want an answer for and now you must put yourself into the head of your future employer and look at it from their perspective. Remember, they will probably consider applications from "2nd round" candidates for no more than 30 seconds to 1 minute. What do you think they want to see in that time?

They certainly *don't* want to read anything that is too hard, complex, incoherent, poorly organized, etc. At this point, they most likely need to determine that you meet ALL of the essential requirements, and many of the desirable ones as specified in the advertisement.

A simple statement such as *"I meet all the essential requirements"* **will not do it**!!! You need a series of strongly constructed statements on your cover letter which state HOW your relevant experience etc meets ALL the requirements... for example, if you needed proven customer handling skills, you could say something like...

"My experience as a Receptionist in a busy Real Estate office over the past two years has allowed me to develop a wide range of skills related to effectively handling customer enquiries and complaints."

Such statements can make more than one point, and often addressing several selection criteria if you are careful in your choice of words.

Round Three...

The 15-25% of applications that make it this far are given very serious consideration to select WHO will come in for an interview.

Out of those original 100 applications received, they'd probably only want to interview the top 5-10. So now the employer will be looking in detail at your complete application. Their attention will go to your attached résumé which demonstrate and reinforce what you stated in your cover letter.

In fact, you will find that you need to do different versions of your résumé to tailor it to suit individual positions you are applying for. Specifically, the area of your résumé which addresses the essential criteria should be reviewed and tweaked every time.

How can you "hide" the fact that you don't have all the essential requirements? Well, if you are lacking in one area, you may be able to emphasize the others a bit more. It all depends on how many of your competitors have addressed all the requirements. In that case, you could be out of luck. It also depends on how strict they are with the screening of those that don't address all the criteria.

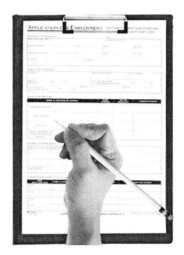

Job Application Forms

Why do employers use job applications? Many employers use them as a way of standardizing the information they obtain from all job-seekers, including some things that you would not normally put on your résumé. Your goal is to complete the application as completely and honestly as you can - all the time remembering that the application is a key marketing tool for you in the job-hunting process. Remember that some employers will use your application as a basis for deciding whether to call you for an interview.

So, armed with this knowledge, here are the ins and outs of completing job applications.

Arrive prepared.

Be sure to bring your résumé, driver's license, etc. You may also need addresses and phone numbers of previous employers, as well as starting and ending dates for each previous job. It's always better if have too much information available than not enough.

Follow instructions carefully.

Always take a few minutes to review the entire application first. Some applications ask for information differently - and all have specific spaces in which you are expected to answer questions. Think of the application as your first test in following instructions.

Be as neat as possible.

Ever wonder why learning handwriting was important in elementary school? Neatness and legibility count; the application is a reflection of you. If completing it by hand, be sure to use only a blue or black pen, not red or glitter or pencil. Think before you start writing so that you have your thoughts organized. Don't fold, bend, or otherwise mar the application. Don't scribble out answers or write them along the side or back. If you need an additional piece of paper to complete your answer, then ask the receptionist for one but try to keep your answer to the space allotted on the form. They usually leave a small space for your answer because they only want to see a high level response with minimal detail. You can explain the detail in the interview.

Tailor your responses.

Just as with your résumé and cover letter, you want to focus your education and experience to the job to which you are applying. Give details of skills and accomplishments, and avoid framing your experiences in terms of mere duties and responsibilities. Show why you are more qualified than other applicants for the position. Include experience from all sources, including previous jobs, school, clubs and organizations, and volunteer work.

Answer all questions.

One of the reasons employers have you complete an application is because they want the same information from all job applicants. However, if there are questions that do not apply to you, simply respond with "not applicable," or "n/a". Do not write "see résumé" when completing the application (but you can certainly attach your résumé to the application). You can give a high level response and add a notation stating "See attached résumé for more detail".

Don't focus on the negative.

As with any job search correspondence, never offer negative information. Your goal with the application is to get an interview. Providing negative information (such as being fired from a job or how many times you have applied to this company without getting an interview) just gives the employer a reason not to interview you.

Always respond truthfully.

The fastest way for an application to be rejected is if it contains a lie. But, keep in mind that it doesn't mean you need to give complete answers either. For example, many applications ask your reason for leaving your last job. If you were fired or you quit without giving two-weeks notice, you might try to write "job completed" as the reason you left your last job and leave longer explanations for the interview.

Do not include your salary requirements.

It is way too early in the job-seeking process to be identified by a specific salary request. You don't want to give employers too much information too soon. In addition, employers often use this question as a screening device - and you don't want to be eliminated from consideration based on your answer. It's best to say "open" or "negotiable." If you are forced to put a specific number, you can try to either add a salary range or you can note "At my last job, I was paid $400 per week" if room on the page will allow.

Provide references only if requested.

Employers want to see that there are people who will provide objective information about you to them. Pick your references carefully - and make sure you ask them if they are willing to be a reference for you before you list them.

Where do you get references? From past employers, teachers, or family friends. Do not use your friends from class as character references or have them pretend to be past employers. Trickery never works. Most young job-seekers have a mix of professional and character references, while more experienced job-seekers focus on professional references who can speak of your skills and accomplishments. Make sure that you have the permission of your reference before using them. As well, don't forget to let them know once you have provided their names to a potential employer. You want to make sure that your reference will be prepared to give you the best recommendation possible.

Your application should be consistent with your résumé.

Make sure all dates, names, titles, etc., on your application correspond with the information on your résumé. Don't worry if the application is based on chronological employment while you have a functional résumé.

Understand the questions before answering.

A common problem when filling in application forms is not understanding (and therefore, not answering) what the question is asking! If you aren't sure what they are asking of you, then continue to the next question and remember to come back to the problem question later. You may be able to think more clearly after gaining some confidence from answering some "easier" questions. If that does not help you, don't be embarrassed to ask the receptionist for clarification.

Proofread before submitting.

Once you've completed the application, sit back and take a moment to thoroughly proofread the document, checking for all errors – especially grammatical errors and misspellings.

Not all application forms are alike.

Be prepared for all kinds of job applications, from simple one-page applications to multi-page applications; and some will be clean and crisp copies while others will appear to be photocopied a few too many times. Regardless, take your time and do the best you can, always keeping in the back of your mind the goal of the application -- getting you an interview.

✎ Exercise: Mix 'n Match

Listed below are two separate groups of terms which are commonly found on application forms.

For each group, you must try to match the term with its correct definition.

GROUP ONE

a. Surname/Family Name

b. Given Names/Other Names

c. Maiden Name/Née/Former Name

d. Preferred Name

e. D.O.B.

f. Home/Residential Address

g. Marital Status

h. Religion

i. Secondary Education

j. Tertiary Education

k. Institutions Attended

l. Dependents

m. Spouse

n. Guardian

o. Disability

1. Your date of birth.

2. High school education.

3. Your wife's/husband's name.

4. Name common to all members of your family.

5. Female's name before marriage.

6. Medical or physical problems.

7. The people who you support financially.

8. Person who looks after you if your parents do not.

9. The name in b which you like to be called.

10. Names of places you went to in i & j.

11. Tech., College or University education.

12. Single, married, widowed, divorced, separated or in a common law relationship - does not have to be completed.

13. The names given to you which make you different from other members of your family.

14. Where you live.

15. You don't need to answer this question.

GROUP TWO

a. Convictions/Offences

1. Time spent in the Army, Navy, Air Force or Reserve Forces.

b. Next of Kin

2. Signed statement saying that all the information given is true and correct.

c. Period of Notice/Availability

3. Previous person or firm you have worked for.

d. References

4. Your closest relative-wife, husband, father, mother, etc.

e. Armed Service

5. Times you've been found guilty of breaking the law.

f. Citizenship

6. People who can tell someone about your character, your professional experience and/or how well you might work.

g. Former Employer

7. Not applicable, doesn't apply to me.

h. Work History/Experience

8. Person's name written (not printed) by him/her self.

i. Place of Birth

9. Amount of time needed before you can start new job and/or leave old one.

j. Mother's Maiden Name

10. What job a person does for a living.

k. Occupation

11. Country/town where you were born.

l. Declaration

12. Country of birth or of naturalisation.

m. Signature

13. Details of the places/jobs you have been employed in.

n. N/A

14. Your mother's surname before she was married.

ANSWERS

Answers to the previous exercise are below...

How did you do?

GROUP ONE

a. Surname/Family Name	4. Name common to all members of your family.
b. Given Names/Other Names	13. The names given to you which make you different from other members of your family.
c. Maiden Name/Nee/Former Name	5. Female's name before marriage.
d. Preferred Name	9. Name in b which you like to be called.
e. D.O.B.	1. Your date of birth.
f. Home/Residential Address	14. Where you live.
g. Marital Status	12. Single, married, widowed, divorced, separated or in a common-law relationship *(does not legally have to be completed)*.
h. Religion	15. Legally, you don't need to answer this question.
i. Secondary Education	2. High school education.
j. Tertiary Education	11. Tech., College or University education.
k. Institutions Attended	10. Names of places you went to in i & j.
l. Dependents	7. People who you support financially.
m. Spouse	3. Your wife's/husband's name.
n. Guardian	8. Person who looks after you if your parents do not.
o. Disability	6. Medical or physical problems. *(does not legally have to be completed)*.

GROUP TWO

a. Convictions/Offences	5. Times you've been found <u>guilty</u> of breaking the law. *(you do not have to include charges dropped or pending charges)*
b. Next of Kin	4. Your closest relative-wife, husband, father, mother, etc.
c. Period of Notice/Availability	9. Amount of time needed before you can start

	new job and/or leave old one.
d. References	6. People who can tell someone about your character, your professional experience and/or how well you might work.
e. Armed Service	1. Any period of time spent in the Army, Navy, Air Force or Reserve Forces.
f. Citizenship	12. Country of birth or of naturalisation.
g. Former Employer	3. Previous person or company you have worked for.
h. Work History/Experience	13. Details of the places/jobs you have been employed in.
i. Place of Birth	11. Country/town where you were born.
j. Mother's Maiden Name	14. Your mother's surname before she married.
k. Occupation	10. What job a person does for a living.
l. Declaration	2. Signed statement saying that all the information given is true and correct.
m. Signature	8. Person's name written (not printed) by him/her self.
n. N/A	7. Not applicable, doesn't apply to me

When filling in application forms, the first thing you should do is read every question <u>before</u> you write anything. Make sure you understand what the question is asking!!!

When you have finished, check everything! Have you answered all the questions, and have you answered them correctly and neatly?

Remember, this form may be your only opportunity to get an interview (which is your goal at this stage) so take it very seriously.

Job Interviews

Employer's Market

While being interviewed for a job; you are focused on making a good impression. What do you think makes a good impression? What do employers look for when interviewing job applicants?

✎Exercise: Put Yourself In The Employer's Shoes...

What things would you look for if you were interviewing someone for a job as a:

- Salesperson?
- Gardener?
- Police Officer?
- Secretary?
- Waiter / Waitress?
- Teacher?
- Illustrator?

Let's think:

What things would you want these people to have / to bring, if *you* were interviewing them for a job?

What items would you **not** want these people to have / to bring, if *you* were interviewing them for a job?

How would you want these people to behave / present themselves?

How would you **not** want these people to behave / present themselves?

Think about the type of questions you would ask them.

What kind of answers would have a positive impact on you?

What kind of answers would make you reject the interviewee immediately?

Every role is different so the questions that an interviewer will ask or documents that s/he would want to see will vary. For example, an illustrator will probably bring work samples where a waitress will not. But a waitress would be prepared to discuss challenging customers where an illustrator may discuss challenging deadlines or projects.

If you try to put yourself in the interviewer's position before you go to the interview, you will be able to better prepare for a successful interview.

✎ Exercise: Mix 'n Match

Listed below are some general things that an employer might look for in job applicants. Can you match the word, with its correct definition?

1. Appearance
2. Speech
3. Anxiety
4. Personality
5. Attitude
6. Enthusiasm
7. Honesty
8. Reliability
9. Confidence
10. Alertness
11. Ambition
12. Interests
13. Skills
14. Work Experience
15. Education
16. Intelligence
17. Character
18. Professionalism
19. Stress Management
20. Collaboration

a) Nervousness, insecurity or uneasy feeling about a situation.

b) What I feel about specific situation, people and/or things.

c) The image that I project by my clothing, grooming and body language.

d) Showing great interest and eagerness in something.

e) The way in which I communicate verbally to others.

f) Things which make me as a likeable and unique person.

g) Having trust or belief in yourself and your abilities.

h) Awake, prepared, attentive and ready to act.

i) Being sincere, truthful and trustworthy.

j) Always ready to share ideas and lend a hand to others.

k) Able to be dependable, consistent and accurate.

l) The things I am good at doing.

m) The knowledge and skills I have gained from school, college, etc.

n) The ways I react in high-pressure situations.

o) Work I have done which may have taught me skills useful to an employer.

p) My ability to act maturely and appropriately when at work.

q) My ability to use my knowledge and my understanding.

r) My feelings about what is right and wrong.

s) My desire to do well - to succeed.

t) The things I enjoy doing most or inspire me.

Answers:

Here are some general things that an employer might look for in job applicants.

1. Appearance — c) The image that I project by my clothing, grooming and body language.

2. Speech — e) The way in which I communicate verbally to others.

3. Anxiety — a) Nervousness, insecurity or uneasy feeling.

4. Personality — f) Things which make me as a likeable and unique person.

5. Attitude — b) How I feel about specific situations, people and/or things.

6. Enthusiasm — d) Showing great interest and eagerness in something.

7. Honesty — i) Being sincere, truthful and trustworthy.

8. Reliability — k) Able to be dependable, consistent and accurate.

9. Confidence — g) Having trust or belief in yourself and your abilities.

10. Alertness — h) Awake, prepared, attentive and ready to act.

11. Ambition — s) My desire to do well - to succeed.

12. Interests — t) The things I enjoy doing most or inspire me.

13. Skills — l) The things I am good at doing.

14. Work Experience — o) Work I have done which may have taught me skills useful to an employer.

15. Education — m) The knowledge and skills I have gained from school, college, etc.

16. Intelligence — q) My ability to use my knowledge and my understanding.

17. Character — r) My feelings about what is right and wrong.

18. Professionalism — p) My ability to act maturely and appropriately when at work.

19. Stress Management — n) The ways that I react in high-pressure situations.

20. Collaboration — j) Always ready to share ideas and lend a hand to others.

Preparing For The Job Interview

What should you try to find out before the interview? What things should you have prepared to take with you? (HINT: your résumé better be on this list!)

Research, Research, Research

Don't assume that because you have been granted an interview that the hard part is over. Actually, it has just begun. To stack the deck in your favour, you should spend some time researching the company, its culture and the interviewers themselves. Learn about the role you are applying for and what they may be looking for in their potential employees.

Being sufficiently prepared will help you to be relaxed and confident during your interview. Just think of it like an exam - how nervous do you feel before an exam that you haven't studied for? The same principle applies to interviews.

Study the role you are applying for. What are the key things they are looking for? What relevant strengths do you possess that meet those needs? This is no time to be modest. Think about what you can offer your employer. Also think about your weaknesses too.

Get to know the company. A little background information can go a long way. Don't just rely on the company's website for information. Try to find the latest Annual Report online or any current articles or press releases about the company in terms of acquisitions, changes in management, awards, volunteer sponsorships and lines of business. While you probably won't be asked direct questions in regard to these topics, you may be asked "what do you know about us?". You must demonstrate during the interview that you have a solid knowledge of the company. It will impress the interviewer(s) and show them that you are interested in them and would fit easily into the company culture.

During the interview, try to take an opportunity to "casually" mention some of your knowledge. For example;

"I was really impressed that Stevenson Mining sponsors the Calgary Women in Business Luncheon every year as I have attended it over the last few years."

"I am excited to hear from the last month's press release that Arctic National Bank is expanding into the Northern Quebec market. Since I am fluently bilingual, I could be of assistance during and after this transition."

"I have strong sales skills, am an excellent team player and am very eager to be involved in the new markets you are developing in the South American region."

If you know the names of any or all of the interviewers, then "Google" them. Try to find out something about them that you can relate to in conversation and show a common interest. For example;

If you find that your interviewer has run a recent marathon, you may want to mention that you are planning on training to participate in a 10K run next year. Or if your interviewer won the company golf tournament, you may want to subtly mention that your hobby is golf. (Only use this tactic if it is true. You never want to be caught in a lie.)

If your interviewer recently won an award or had a baby, you may want to congratulate him / her.

⊘ **Tip**: Be careful of which topics you bring up. Don't bring up any private, political, religious or legal issues no matter how involved your interviewer may be in those activities.

Try to be sensitive to areas that you may not be aware, for example, don't ask your interviewer about their personal life no matter how harmless it may seem. There is nothing worse than asking about someone's family member or pet and finding out from the reaction that his/her mother or 18 year old dog just died. Don't ask about family life either unless you have specific knowledge from a networking connection in this area. Again, an interviewer will not look kindly upon you if you ask about their spouse and you find out that he/she is going through a messy divorce.

Don't ever let your guard down and be too casual. While you should feel free to talk about how you and your interviewer went to the same University but don't brag about your award for drinking more tequila shots than anyone else in your fraternity / sorority.

The goal is to create a comfort and familiarity between you and your interviewer. You want to be able to create some relaxing chit-chat. If you succeed at that, then you have a better chance at getting the job. Remember, interviewers are not only looking for someone who can do the job but also someone that they can get along with.

Plan your wardrobe

How you present yourself will show how professional you are and how well you will fit in. Look at the clothes you own now...

✎ Exercise: What to wear?

What would you wear for a job interview as:
- An Office Worker?
- A Plumber's Trainee?
- A Flight Attendant?
- A Gardener?
- A Daycare Assistant?
- A Receptionist in a retirement home?

Let's think…

Would you wear the same clothes for each interview? Why? Why not?

Could you wear sandals or open shoes for any interview? Stilettos? Thigh-high boots?

Should females wear a bra? Leather skirt? Low-cut sweater?

Should males wear a tie? Golf shorts? Jeans? Running Shoes?

What factors decide what you should or should not wear for a job interview?

Key things to remember when selecting your interview wardrobe:

☒ Don't dress sexy or flashy.	☑ Do dress modestly, i.e. cover up.
☒ Don't dress like a slob.	☑ Do wear clothes that are clean and pressed.
☒ Don't wear items that are fraying, missing buttons or have holes.	☑ Do wear tailored (but not tight) outfits.
☒ Don't look like you just rolled out of your hamper. Your clothes will probably smell like it as well.	☑ Do wear something that makes you feel confident. If you are unsure that an outfit is appropriate, don't wear it!
☒ Don't wear an outfit that you wore when you were in Grade 6.	☑ Do make sure your outfit is appropriate for the job.

Remember, you don't have to have a designer suit or the latest trends to impress. You can wear something simple as long as it looks like it fits and it is clean. If you don't have anything suitable, borrow from your friends or siblings. The right wardrobe will make all the difference in the world. (More about this topic later.)

Manners

Always be polite not just during the interview but to any one you may have contact with in the office or work environment.   Some companies will purposely have you wait in the reception area for an extended period so that the receptionist can secretly observe your behaviour and interaction with others.

Punctuality

One of the <u>biggest</u> turn offs for any employer is lateness!

To make sure you aren't late... if the interview is for 10.00am, should you turn up:
- at 9.30am
- at 9.45am
- at 10.00am
OR at some other time?

Let's think...

If you are unsure of the location (i.e. you've never been to that building or part of town before), would you investigate where it is first? How would you do this?

Think of a place approximately 10 kilometres from your home.

How long would it take you to get there?

How would you get there?

What is your Plan "B" in the event of some emergency such as a flat tire or heavy traffic or missing a bus / train connection?

Always carry the phone number of the interviewer with you in case you will be late. Proper etiquette is to inform them if you know that you will be late.

Arriving At Your Job Interview

Let's think...

What should you do when you get there?

Is it a good idea to make a good impression with the receptionist? Why? Why not?

What would you say to the receptionist? How would you greet him / her?

Would you ask the receptionist any questions? Why? Why not? What questions?

If you have to wait, what could you be doing to pass the time?

Would it be appropriate to smoke, eat or make phone calls while you are waiting?

Should you turn your cell phone off before the interview?

Should you look at your Blackberry during your interview?

During Your Job Interview

Do you know what to do in different situations?

Shaking hands

Should you shake hands with the interviewer?

Absolutely. Make sure that your hands are clean and dry. Don't have a dirty tissue in your hands either. Also never clean your hands with sanitizer right after the handshake unless you want to insult your prospective employer.

What type of hand-shaker are you?

How you shake hands with someone can impact their first impression of you. Do you shake hands like a:

Crusher? – You squeeze so hard that your victim's blood flow stops and their bones start cracking. You appear as overly aggressive and over-powering.

Mover & Shaker? – Your grip is good but you shake too briskly and never let go. You give the impression as having too much caffeine or being very nervous.

Limp Fish? – You are barely grasping your interviewer's hand. You give the impression that you lack confidence and are disinterested.

Firm? – You grasp your interviewer's hand with some firmness but not too tight and smile. This is the ideal grip as it makes the interviewer see you as confident and eager.

Sitting down

Is it appropriate to wait until you are asked to sit? If you aren't asked, what can you do?

You should try to mirror your interviewer and wait until s/he starts to sit. Always try to follow his/her lead. It will give the impression that you are in sync with him / her.

Addressing the employer

How should you address the interviewer?

Sir? Madam? Jimmy? Mr. Baxter? Buddy?

If you have spoken to the interviewer before, you can address him / her by his / her first name, unless he gives you an indication that s/he prefers to be more formal.

Wait until s/he introduces him/herself. If s/he uses her/his first name, then it is acceptable to address him/her in this regard. Otherwise, you can ask if it is okay to call him/her by his/her first name. If s/he introduces her/himself as "Jim Smythe" or "Julie Manon", then address him/her formally (i.e. use "Mr." or "Ms.") until you are corrected otherwise. Better to be too formal than too informal. At least you will be showing respect.

What can you do if you don't know or can't remember the person's name?

Try to shape your conversation where you don't have to use his/her name. At the end of the interview, ask for a business card so that you may contact him if you have any questions. This way, you can use his/her name as you say goodbye and you are able to send a "thank-you" letter.

Handing over your credentials

At what stage should you present your credentials (résumé, references, etc.) to the interviewer? Is discussing your credentials sufficient?

When you meet your interviewer, look him or her directly (but not aggressively!) in the eyes and offer a firm handshake. Smile and greet the person by name. If possible, make a little small talk. A comment or two about the weather is usually a safe topic.

Once you sit down, you may offer to hand over your résumé. Usually, the interviewer will have a copy but they are always appreciative when you offer. If you have references or work samples, hold on to them until they come up in conversation. If the interviewer does not inquire about them, then offer to provide them at the end of the interviewer or whenever you feel it is appropriate within the conversation.

During the interview, answer succinctly. This means don't ramble about stuff unrelated to the question. Be brief and answer the question clearly. If you need a moment or two to gather your thoughts, simply say you need to think about the question for a moment. Your honesty will be appreciated. Just don't drag on the thoughtful moment for too long.

Be sure to show interest in the company by asking questions at appropriate times during the interview. End the interview by thanking the interviewer for his or her time.

Don't chew gum. Gum chewing is a major turn-off for employers. Imagine what your interviewer would think if when you opened her mouth to respond to the first question and a bright pink piece of bubble gum flies out of your mouth and hits the interviewer's notepad.

Answering Job Interview Questions

Questions will probably be asked in a rapid sequence, and can be designed to put pressure on the applicant. In some cases, you will be interviewed by more than one person – your potential future manager, a member of the team, HR or even someone not related to the job. Usually, for higher positions, you may be interviewed by a panel of people.

Your goal of the interview is not only to articulate what you stated on your résumé, but you need to show that you are a perfect fit – in personality, work ethic, teamwork, as well as skills.

If you have sensible answers prepared which you can present confidently, you will be well on your way to making a strong impression. Don't downplay your previous experience, no matter how lowly it may seem. All of these are transferable experiences. Transferable skills from any of these jobs could include being flexible, creative, a good communicator, promptness, handling money, responding to customer feedback, setting and keeping a schedule, as well as balancing schoolwork with other activities.

Avoid peppering interviews with "um" and "like."

The best way to get past overusing these "pause words" is practice. As you conduct practice interviews with friends and family, have them flag you if you start inserting too many "um's" and "like's" into your interview responses.

Be memorable (in a positive way).

One tip is to have a visual trademark such as a unique lapel pin. You could find a pin that represents a hobby you have, such as a sailboat or a tennis racket. Then, when the interviewer asks what kinds of pastimes you enjoy, you can link the pin into the conversation. Later, when the interviewer is narrowing down the herd, you are sure to stand out. Don't wear anything political, religious, juvenile (i.e. South Park) or questionable (i.e. hunting, union, anti-union). Don't be too flashy either. You don't want your level of taste questioned.

Show your enthusiasm.

Employers list lack of enthusiasm as their No. 1 turnoff in interviewees. The best way to show enthusiasm? A big natural smile throughout the interview. But not one of those psycho-zombie smiles, but one that looks more like you are singing "Happy Birthday" for your best friend.

Project confidence.

The scary world of job interviewing is new to teens and new graduates, but overcoming the fear and appearing confident is a great way to stand out. Teen girls are especially vulnerable to appearing timid in interviews because they sometimes lapse into using "little girl" voices. One of the best ways to show confidence is with a strong, confident voice. No matter how shaky you may feel inside, try your best to show a confident attitude.

Types of Questions That You May Be Asked

There are various types of questions that you can be asked to get the information that the hiring manager needs from you in order to make an informed decision. Each style of question elicits different types of answers depending on the requirements of the job. As you interview for more advanced jobs, you will see more of these types of interview questions which is why you should really know your résumé inside and out.

Behavioural

Behavioural questions ask you to draw on specific events from your past work history or experiences. They enable the interviewer to assess how you will perform on the job. The more recent and the more frequent the behaviour, the greater the predictive power.

Sample questions:

- Describe a situation in which you were able to use persuasion to successfully convince someone to see things your way.

- Give me an example of a time when you set a goal and were able to meet or achieve it.

- Give me a specific example of a time when you had to conform to a policy with which you did not agree.

- Tell me about a recent situation in which you had to deal with a very upset customer or co-worker.

- Tell me about a time when you had to go above and beyond the call of duty in order to get a job done.

Situational

As with Behavioural questions, this technique can be used for applicants with either extensive or minimal work experience. They take the form of hypothetical questions based on situations likely to be encountered in this position. Usually they are used if the position requires a solution-focused approach or if you have minimal experience.

Sample questions:

- If you feel yourself getting overwhelmed at work by the volume of change, what coping strategies do you use to get yourself back on track?

- What would you do if someone higher in the organization instructed you to do something that was illegal or unethical?

- A project is given to you and in your analysis you found out that the project cannot be completed in time as per the specification. What would you do and how will you convey your message?

- How would you handle believing strongly in a recommendation you made in a meeting, but most of your co-workers shot it down?
- What would you do if the priorities on a project you were working on changed suddenly?

Technical/Credential

These questions are used to determine whether or not you have the particular skill or knowledge required to perform the duties of the position. They are useful where specific knowledge; skill sets and experience are required to perform the minimum requirements.

Sample questions:
- How do you keep abreast of changes in…Industry? Legislations? Software? Updates?
- What are two methods of retrieving SQL Data?
- Can you please tell me about your experience with…?
- When did you complete your XXX designation? Where did you take your courses?
- Define Data Abstraction. What is its importance?

Variation of Technical

These types of puzzles or brainteasers are famous for being used extensively in IT interviews for Google and Microsoft. Sometimes they will use technical brainteasers that make you write code in the interview (assuming you are going for a job as a programmer). Even trickier, they may use questions that have no answer. This is not common unless they need a superhero in technical expertise or the job entails a large amount of stress. But some of these types of questions can be fun especially if there is no right answer.

Since the interviewer who poses these questions is looking to learn about your thinking process, don't just shout out the answer or "I don't know". Talk out the problem out loud to show them how you arrived at the answer or where you got stuck.

Sample questions:
1. A man has to get a fox, a chicken, and a sack of corn across a river. He has a rowboat, and it can only carry him and one other thing. If the fox and the chicken are left together, the fox will eat the chicken. If the chicken and the corn are left together, the chicken will eat the corn. How does the man do it?
2. You have been assigned to design Bill Gates' bathroom. Naturally, cost is not a consideration. You may not speak to Bill. How would you go about it?
3. If you are going to receive an award in 5 years, what is it for and who is the audience?
4. You have to explain Microsoft Excel to your grandma. How would you do it?
5. Why are manhole covers round?

<u>Answers to some of the above:</u>

Fox/Chicken/Grain – Man goes across with chicken and comes back. Goes across with Fox. Picks up Chicken and brings it back and leaves it on original bank. Picks up grain and goes across and leaves it with fox. Goes back and retrieves chicken.

Manhole covers: Round because one person can transport by rolling. Square ones can fall in on the diagonal. Less material needed for round. Etc....

Open-ended Questions

Open-ended questions allow the interviewer to get a feel for your personality and professionalism as well as your verbal communication skills. They are used in conjunction with other more structured interview questions. Interviewers use open ended questions related to general experience in the workplace, education, contributions they can make to the position, etc.

Open-ended questions are best used to put you at ease at the beginning of the interview and can have a similar effect closing off the structured questions with a more casual and friendly approach.

Sample questions:

- Why are you interested in this position?
- What skills do you think you could bring to this position?
- Please expand on the roles and responsibilities you held during your last position?
- What makes a job interesting to you?
- What qualities do you feel a successful manager should have?

Common Interview Questions

Here are some other possible interview questions and responses that you may find helpful in your preparation.

What are your strengths and weaknesses?

Always give strengths relevant to the position you are going for. Some stand-out strengths employers are looking for are:

- ☑ Easily adaptable.
- ☑ Quick learner.
- ☑ Works well as part of a team.
- ☑ Self motivated.
- ☑ Hard working.
- ☑ Eager to learn.
- ☑ Ability to work well under pressure.
- ☑ Strong communication skills.
- ☑ Willingness to pitch in without being asked.

In terms of weaknesses be honest if you feel there is something relevant that you want to improve on then let your employer know how you have resolved this weakness. It will show the ability to self reflect which is a strength. Plus it also shows that this is no longer a weakness that they need to be concerned with.

Always make sure that you emphasize the steps that you have taken to improve on it. For example, "I've had trouble delegating duties to others because I felt I could do things better myself. This has sometimes backfired because I'd end up with more than I could handle and the quality of my work would suffer. But I've taken courses in time management and learned effective delegation techniques, and I feel I've overcome this weakness."

Be sure the weakness you talk about is <u>not</u> a key element of the position or reflective of poor conduct. For example, don't use these:

"I have a weakness for the ladies."

"I tend to ignore deadlines. Maybe I should take a course when I am less busy."

"I have trouble getting out of bed in the morning especially after binge drinking the night before."

"I don't really get along with people too well. But I work great on my own."

"I tend not to give the customers what they ask for but I give them what I think they need so they should be happy."

What experience do you have, if any?

Answers to this question should be based firstly on experience relevant to the position, then any other experience of interest. This does not have to be paid work. If you lack experience in the area, you can present other experiences as examples such as sporting situations – these can show leadership skills as well as working within a team unit, commitment, dedication and goal setting.

Use school activities as they show diversity and work ethic. For example, if you are interviewing to be a Customer Service Representative on an IT Help Desk, you can use your experience on the school dance committee. In that role, you had to understand clearly people's wants and understand previous event planning failures. You may add that your strong communications skills allowed you to lead the discussion to a collaborative solution.

What do you want to do when you finish school?

It is important even if you're not sure of your future career goals to present some sort of direction. Going on to university, working within the industry you are applying to or just setting some goals.

If this is the field that you are interested in, then mention it and discuss why. Don't be fake nor too detailed and longwinded.

What are you other commitments? e.g. sport, school activities etc.

Now outside commitments can work either way depending on the nature of the job. It is important to be honest about serious commitments such as schoolwork. In terms of sports and other activities this will all depend on how serious you are about them. Be flexible when talking in terms of availability but also let your employer know if you have commitments you can't or are not willing to break.

Don't bring up controversial religious or political activities, for example, you can say "I volunteer for my local MP", not "I am actively working on a petition to legalize pot and abolish abortion". Employers will not hire someone who may stir the pot whether they agree with your personal passions or not.

How quickly do you adapt to new situations?

Ideally employers are looking for people who can adapt quickly and are versatile. Discuss an example such as if you moved to a new neighbourhood as a child or your experience adapting to university.

You should discuss the change in situations, the challenges you have encountered and how you overcame those challenges.

Are you able to work to a deadline?

You have a proven ability to work to deadlines as you have been doing it at school. Meeting assignment deadlines is a good way to show employers you can work to time constraints. An example is "As a member of the Student Council, I was given only 2 weeks to set up a student body assembly with guest speakers to commemorate Women's History Month." Always mention the goal, the challenges and how you overcame them to make it a success.

How do you feel about school?

Whether you love it or hate it, it is best to stay positive. You don't have to be over the top. Just try to think of some things you like about it. You can talk about challenges that stimulated you, different people you have met, or focus on subjects or clubs that you liked and why.

Don't complain or belittle it!

Do you prefer to work alone or as part of a team?

It would be beneficial to say you are capable of doing both. Depending on the position you might be required to be by yourself or you could be part of a team. Be flexible. You need to show you can function in both environments.

Talk about positive experiences that you have had working on a team but also mention that you are very capable of working with "minimal supervision".

How do you deal with conflict situations?

Conflict in the workplace should always be dealt with professionally and calmly. If you were unable to deal with the situation yourself you would notify someone who could. For example, you might discuss a time when there was a disagreement on a school committee or team and how it was resolved.

Don't get personal and point the finger at someone and accuse them of being stupid, unreasonable or ridiculous. You want to show that you are a diplomat and not a brat that must get his/her own way.

Don't forget to discuss the resolution and your contribution. If you convince someone else to see the situation your way, discuss how you achieved this. For example, "I did some research and showed the committee a comparison of results from different fundraising efforts in the past 5 years to show that car washes are not as successful as 50-50 draws."

If you compromised, discuss how and why you came to this result and how your negotiation or diplomacy skills were used. For example, "I coached a Little League team and one of our players refused to run for the ball in the outfield. The team wanted me to bench him because he was causing a lot of unnecessary runs being scored. So, one day after practice, I took the player aside and went for a slice of pizza. After some chit-chat, he told me that he wants to play third base and no one is giving him a chance. So, I agreed to have him try it in practice and he played very well. We agreed that he would have a chance to play third base in a game but there will be times when we needed him in the outfield. He agreed to compromise and performed both roles. Because he felt that he was being valued, he played outfield with greater energy and enthusiasm. The rest of the team was happier as well and the harmony on the team was restored. We ended up having a winning season that year and received a third place trophy."

How do you handle stressful situations?

Give some examples of stressful situations you've dealt with in the past. Tell them how you use time management, problem-solving or decision-making skills to reduce stress. For example, tell them that making a "to-do" list to keep organized and help you prioritize has helped you. Cite stress-reducing techniques such as stretching and taking a break. Don't be afraid to admit that you will ask for assistance if you are feeling overwhelmed.

Feel free to say that you actually work better under pressure if it is true. But be sure that you don't look like a risk taker or disorganized.

Tell me a little about yourself.

This is the most common question used. It is a great ice-breaker. More importantly, it is a great opportunity to market you as an excellent fit for the job, team and company. This is not the time to talk about your personal life (i.e. "I was born at 5:03am in a small shack in the remote woods of Northern Ontario…"). This question is deliberately vague to see how you understand the requirements of the job and how it is a match with your background within 30 seconds.

Always be honest, but talk about your best traits only, especially those that relate to the position for which you are applying. Highlight experiences and accomplishments you are most proud of.

✐ **Hint**: Stick to this format so that you don't lose this opportunity:

a) *Introduce yourself.* "My name is ….."

b) *Tell what your current status is (i.e. last job title or student status).* "I am currently a Senior at Central Tech High School but have worked part-time as a Sales Associate at the Rocky Mountain Chocolate Factory for 2 years."

c) *Describe what you do at work (or school).* "I work on a very busy front counter answering customers' questions about our products, making recommendations and processing purchases. As well, I am responsible for making various types of candy apples and chocolate specialties."

d) *Describe one or two things you've accomplished or excel at that directly relate to the position.* "Since I have started at the store, sales have increased 10% during my shifts because I am able to use my extensive knowledge of our products and my strong customer service skills to help customers make the best purchases for them. In addition, I have created new candy apple products that incorporated various holiday celebrations for the store's diverse ethnic communities. In the first year, the store's candy apple sales soared by 45% as a result."

e) *Mention why you decided to apply for this position.* "I have been accepted to Ryerson's prestigious Marketing program and am planning a career in Product Development and Brand Management so I think working as an Administrative Assistant in your Consumer Product Testing department would be a great fit."

Example:

My name is Ainsley Bosworth (a), and I'm a senior at Central Tech High School (b) where I'm preparing to go to college for kinesiology (c). I have worked part-time as an Assistant Personal Trainer at Silver's Gym. I'm very comfortable with public speaking, and I've been a group leader on several school projects (d). I want to get closer to the subject of physical therapy, so I think being the receptionist in a doctor's sports rehabilitation office would be a good step for me (e).

Remember to tailor your response to the specific job. By studying the job announcement, you'll get a good idea of the skills and experience being sought. Work those into your response. But don't drone on-and-on and bore your audience.

Consider this your own personal 30 second commercial. If the interview consisted of only this ONE chance to sell yourself, what would you say?

Finally there are a few questions that employers are not permitted to ask. These are questions pertaining to religion, gender, sexuality, race, relationship status, and ethnicity. It is important to be aware that you do not have to answer questions of this nature. For more information, visit http://www.jobpostings.ca/resource.cfm?id=68.

✎ Exercise: Anticipate Interview Questions

Look closely at each of these other questions.

Try to work out **what** the interviewer might be looking for, and then **prepare your answers** to the questions.

Practice saying your answers so that you will sound confident when you are with the interviewer.

- What were your best subjects at school?
- What hobbies do you enjoy doing?
- Why do you want to do this job?
- How did you decide to pick this type of work?
- What do you know about this job?
- What do you know about our firm?
- What plans do you have for the future?
- What type of work experience have you had?
- Tell me about yourself . . .
- What are your strong/weak points?
- How do you spend your spare time?
- Why did you choose the subjects you did at school?
- Why don't you have a job?
- Why do you want to work for us?
- Have you applied for jobs with other companies?
- How would you behave if you didn't get on with your boss or other workers?
- What do you hope to achieve from this job?
- What do you think success is?
- How well do you carry out instructions?
- What do you see yourself doing in five years time?
- What are you looking for in life?
- Why should we employ you?

If you have had other jobs before, add these possible questions:

- What do you look for in a company?
- Why are you leaving/have you left, your present job?
- How long do you plan to stay with us?
- What do you think of your boss?
- What do you think of your present company?
- Why have you changed jobs so many times?
- Why haven't you changed jobs so far?
- Can you work under pressure?

✍ Exercise: Good Answer or Bad

State what is good OR bad about each **answer** to each of these questions. What reaction is the interviewer likely to have to each response?

Why did you choose this job/career?

- I've always enjoyed being with people and I thought being a receptionist would suit me.
- It was the only thing I could get into at the time.
- I wanted a job in which I could us my hands to make things.
- My father was a banker and he always expected me to follow in his footsteps.
- It pays well, doesn't it?
- I didn't get into medicine or law.
- I felt it was an area in which I could contribute to the world.
- It has good holidays.
- I like working with cars and get great satisfaction from fixing them.
- I think this type of job offers me much scope for variety.

Why do you want to leave your present job?

- I have enjoyed my time at IBM, but I feel it is time to move on to new challenges.
- I hated it there-they made me work too hard.
- I find that my main interest is in selling. Working at EDS doesn't offer much scope in that area.
- I would like to get out before they sack me.
- I would like to work with a smaller firm because I feel it would give me more experience.
- I'm bored there.
- I think I deserve more pay.
- I want to move to Darwin because my girlfriend is here.
- I think this firm needs me.
- I'm happy where I am but I think working here would be even better.

How long would you stay with us?

- I haven't thought that much about it.
- I'm sure my future lies in a firm such as this.
- Probably until I find something better.
- I would like to settle into the job for at least four years and see how things go from there.
- I value security in a job so I would like to stay with the firm for a long time.
- That obviously depends on how things go-whether I'm suited to the firm and the firm to me, but I'd like to think that it would be at least five or six years.
- Until I get pregnant. Have you got a maternity leave plan?
- As long as I'm enjoying working and contributing something useful to your firm.
- Most probably until I retire.
- Who knows???

What are your weaknesses?

- I haven't really got any.

- I do have a tendency to get impatient with inefficiency, but I try not to let it affect my work.

- I've never really thought much about it.

- I steal things.... sometimes.

- I would like to be more organized in some things, such as....

- I'm shy when I first meet people but I can relax after a while.

- I don't think that I have any significant weaknesses which could affect my job, but I do have to be careful not to hurt people with my honest approach.

- I don't know... what are yours?

- I'm a little slow in adapting to new things.

- I'm a failure. I really can't do anything right.

- My mom says that I'm lazy. I'm not. I'm just not a morning person.

Red Flags For The Interviewer

Don't be arrogant or flippant when answering interview questions. Any experienced Hiring Manager will be on the lookout for answers that raise a red flag and let him/her that you are not serious or mature enough. Here are some sample questions and actual inappropriate answers given in interviews:

Question	Red Flag
Tell me about yourself.	"It was a cold February morning when the doctor placed me in my mother's arms for the first time..." **OR** "I am awesome....." (don't brag, keep focus on results /deliverables/ challenges, etc.)
Why do you want to work here?	"I've maxed out three credit cards and need a pay cheque ASAP."
How would others describe you?	"They would say I'm the best you'll meet and you'd be stupid not to hire me."
Why did you leave your last job?	"Gee, there were so many reasons I got out of that hell-hole."
I need someone quickly. If you are selected, when can you start?	If the person is currently employed, regardless of urgency, the employee should say that it would be unfair to just walk out on their current employer and that they feel obligated to give 2 weeks' notice.

Asking Questions In A Job Interview

In any interview, you are expected to ask questions of the interviewer.

An interview is not just a place where they try to find out if you are suited to the job, but also for you to find out if the job suits you. However, the focus of your questions should be worded as to show that you are a benefit to their team and that you are interested in the job, not the perks.

The only way to do that is to ask sensible questions - don't just sit there as if you know everything!

For example, don't ask questions such as these:

- ☒ Can I install different anti-virus software on the server?
- ☒ How often do I get paid?
- ☒ Do I get an office?

At what stage of the interview - start, middle, end, other should you ask questions? Why?

Generally, once the interviewer is done with his/her questions, s/he will ask you if you have any questions. This is the typical flow of the interview conversation. However, if you have relevant questions to the conversation or you need clarification, you can ask questions earlier in the interview. Just be sure that they are on topic, don't detract from the flow of the conversation and demonstrate that you are being insightful and interested.

✎ Exercise: Rephrasing

Could you rephrase any of the "not so strong" questions included below?

- ✐ What type of salary goes with the job?
- ✐ What's the boss like?
- ✐ Would the job involve much travelling?
- ✐ How much does the Managing Director get?
- ✐ What's the latest in office gossip?
- ✐ How quickly could I get to the top?
- ✐ Should I join a union?
- ✐ Do you mind much if employees are late for work?
- ✐ What type of training do you have?
- ✐ Will I have time off to attend any lectures?

What Are Good Interview Questions To Ask?

Confused as to some good "questions" that people should ask in a job interview? There will be a point during the interview when the interviewer will ask you for any questions that you may have. Many applicants sit there in cold stony silence which is automatically giving up an opportunity to

1. Reinforce your fit for the role.
2. Investigate if this role will be a fit for you.

A thoughtful question will show the interviewer that you are engaged in the conversation, that you are intelligent, and that you can act professionally under stress.

An interview is a two-way street. It is designed for you to find out information about the job and working environment too. So... want an idea of the sort of questions you could ask?

Then have a look at this selection, it should give you some ideas of what you can ask!

- ☑ Why is the position open?
- ☑ What happened to the person who previously held this position?
- ☑ Is this a new position?
- ☑ How long has the position been open?
- ☑ Can you describe the work environment here?
- ☑ Can you tell me more about my day-to-day responsibilities?
- ☑ How soon are you looking to fill this position?
- ☑ I have really enjoyed meeting with you and your team, and I am very interested in the opportunity. I feel my skills and experience would be a good match for this position. What is the next step in your interview process?
- ☑ Before I leave, is there anything else you need to know concerning my ability to do this job?
- ☑ In your opinion, what is the most important contribution that this company expects from its employees?
- ☑ Can you please tell me a little bit about the people with whom I'll be working most closely?
- ☑ If you hired me, what would be my first assignment?
- ☑ What is the organization's plan for the next five years, and how does this department or division fit in?
- ☑ What specific skills from the person you hire would make your life easier?
- ☑ What are some of the skills and abilities you see as necessary for someone to succeed in this job?
- ☑ What would be a positive thing the new person could do in first 90 days?
- ☑ What challenges might I encounter if I take on this position?
- ☑ What are your major concerns that need to be immediately addressed in this job?
- ☑ What have you liked most about working here?
- ☑ What are the department's goals, and how do they align with the company's mission?
- ☑ Would you describe for me the actions of a person who previously achieved success in this position?

☑ Would you describe for me the action of a person who previously performed poorly in this position?

☑ How would you describe your own management style?

☑ What personal qualities or characteristics do you most value?

Important: You should <u>never</u> ask about specific compensation or "doing your own thing". This shows total self-interest and arrogance.

Non-Verbal Communication

Even without saying anything, we are able to communicate a lot of information to other people.

The way we walk, sit, stand, hold our hands, use facial expressions and hand gestures and what we wear can tell a trained observer quite a bit about what type of person we are.

✍ Exercise: Speaking without speaking

Look closely at each situation listed below.

Each situation below could be a non-verbal communication to an interviewer. S/he could interpret the situation as listed. (Do not assume that s/he will assume in your favour.)

Review each situation and, if the other reasons applied to you, how would you go about (convincingly) telling the interviewer what is actually happening?

1. Wore good jeans to an interview

a)   Doesn't care much for an office position.

b)   Nicest pants that the person owns.

c)   The good pants have a gaping hole.

2. Just had a haircut the day before the interview

a)   Normally not so tidy - had haircut just for interview.

b)   Had to get the gum out somehow.

c)   Has one every six weeks - including yesterday.

3. Arrived late

a)   Disorganized or doesn't care.

b)   The bus broke down.

c)   Got caught in heavy traffic.

4. Wore brand new clothes to the interview

a)   Done especially to impress us? Hmmm . . .

b)   Had to buy something that was good enough to wear.

c)   Like to look good in new clothes all the time

5. **Very nervous and can't calm down**

   a)   Not prepared . . . too jittery to work for us.

   b)   Prepared . . . but just can't beat the nerves.

   c)   Addicted to Tim Horton's new Turkish Blend?

6. **Doesn't really appear positive and keen**

   a)   Doesn't seem interested enough in the job.

   b)   Know s/he hasn't got a chance anyway.

   c)   Trying to appear cool, but it's not working.

7. **Didn't sit straight in chair**

   a)   Lazy. Used to lying on the couch.

   b)   Got a back problem . . .

   c)   These chairs are terribly uncomfortable.

8. **Didn't look at interviewer - gazed out the window all the time**

   a)   Very shy. Or have they got something to hide?

   b)   The view of the lake is just beautiful!

   c)   Yuk! . . . What an ugly person!

9. **Only occasionally looked at me**

   a)   Why is s/he ignoring me?

   b)   It's a bit hard looking at all three interviewers at once.

   c)   It embarrasses him/her to look directly at people.

10. **Appeared to be overly friendly**

   a)   Too easy-going and casual, has little respect for authority.

   b)   May have overdone the 'be confident' approach.

   c)   Normally easy-going. Able to talk to anyone.

Body Language

The biggest form of non-verbal communication is body language – what your posture and mannerisms reveal what you are thinking (usually without you knowing it). Be wary of how your body language appears.

Here is a list of common interpretations of specific body language demonstrations.

Body language	Possible Interpretation
Standing with hands on hips	Readiness, aggression
Arms crossed on chest	Defensiveness, lacks confidence
Leaning back and crossing arms	Arrogance, condescending
Touching, slightly rubbing nose	Rejection, doubt, lying
Rubbing the eye or looking down, face turned away	Doubt, disbelief
Hands clasped behind back	Anger, frustration, apprehension
Sitting with hands clasped behind head, legs crossed	Confidence, superiority
Tilted head or direct eye contact	Interest, confidence
Patting/fondling hair	Lack of self-confidence; insecurity
Sitting with legs crossed, foot kicking slightly	Boredom
Lack of Eye contact	Lack of confidence
Shifty Eyes	Lying or insecurity
Not answering the questioner	Serious bias issues
Slouching	Disinterest, avoidance
Fidgeting	Discomfort, can't handle stress
Distraction	Arrogance, condescending

🖋 Exercise: An Interview Dialogue

Read through this outline of the responses of three applicants (A, B & C) to the same questions asked of them in an interview.

Consider their answers carefully.

Good morning, my name is Ms. Moffat. You've applied for the Laboratory Assistant's position right?

   A. Yes.

   B. Yes Ms. Moffat, I have.

   C. Yes Ms. Moffat. When I saw it advertised, I thought it would really suit me.

Can you tell me why you replied to our posting?

   A. I .... I 'm not really sure .... ummm ....

   B. Well, I've always enjoyed science and felt that this position would offer me an opportunity to extend my skills in this area.

   C. I think that I'd be really good at this kind of work. In fact, I learn so fast that I'd be looking for promotion very shortly.

Do you know exactly what you would be doing as a Laboratory Assistant?

   A. Well, I don't really know for sure but I think it's got something to do with helping out the scientists in the lab, doesn't it?

   B. A Laboratory Assistant helps to maintain scientific equipment, keeping a check on the supplies in the store, and preparing the chemicals for experiments.

   C. Oh, a Lab. Assistant helps make sure that all the experiments are done okay.

What sort of student do you regard yourself as . . . did you enjoy studying while you were at school?

   A. I wasn't the best student. I didn't really like study all that much but I did it when I had to.

   B. I suppose I'm a reasonable student. I passed all my tests and enjoyed studying subjects that interested me.

   C. I'm a really great student. I didn't have to study much because I always seemed to get by without worrying too much about it.

What were your favourite subjects at school?

   A. I liked Math - it was O.K. . . well, at least the bits I understood were O.K.

   B. Maths and Science were my favourite subjects at school. I also enjoyed doing History.

   C. I'm afraid that I only liked the ones I was good at. The others were so boring that I found them to be a thorough waste of my time.

Do you have any plans for further education?

A. I hadn't really thought much about it . . . I don't know what courses I could do.

B. Well, I've thought about doing the part-time Paralegal Certificate course at Superior Legal College. I think I would really benefit from doing that.

C. Well, if I was forced to do it I suppose I would. But now that I've finished school, I'd much rather try to get my social life back into full swing again.

Suppose our company wanted you to attend a training program to strengthen your skills.... How would you feel about this?

A. Attend a what?

B. If the course would help me improve my potential for promotion and help me to be better at my job I would definitely do it.

C. Attend a course? When? I hope it would be in the day time? Would I get time off from work to attend it? I hope it's not at night - my social life would be ruined. I hope there isn't a test.

Have you ever had a job before?

A. No I haven't. I've never really been into getting one.

B. Yes. I have worked part-time at a take-out restaurant-the one just round the corner. . .

C. No. I've really been too busy. What with all the studying that I've had to do to get maintain my "A" average. . .

We have a lot of other applicants for this position. Why do you think that you deserve to get the job?

A. I dunno - I suppose I'm no different from most other people.

B. I've found out a lot about this type of work and my research suggests that I would be quite capable of doing the work involved because of my experience in my previous job.

C. I guess I'd probably be the best applicant you're likely to get for the job.

Now, do you have any questions you'd like to ask me about the position?

A. No thank you. I don't think so.

B. Yes. Ms. Moffat, could you tell me if this position is new or has it been recently vacated?

C. Yes. . . What's the pay like and how soon until I get my first raise? Do I get an iPhone?

I think I have asked you everything I wanted to. Thank you for coming along to the interview.

A. Thank you Ms. Moffat. Goodbye.

B. Thank you. What is the next step in the process?

C. Oh, think nothing of it. . . Could I see where I'll be working?

✎ Exercise: Rate the Applicants

For each applicant above, choose three words/phrases from the list below, which best describes their answers to the interviewer's questions.

Applicant A ....

Applicant B ....

Applicant C ....

Has done some research	Confident and prepared	Ill-prepared
Unsure	Arrogant	Hesitant
Doubts ability to cope	Lazy	Not interested in the job
An upstart (presumptuous)	Modest but secure	Adequate
Pushy	Polite	Rude
Interested	Keen	Under confident
Energetic	Has good study habits	Has sound attitude to study

Which applicant do you think would be successful? Why?

Getting the Job You Want

How can you be sure you get the job you want? Here are a few tips, especially for teens and young adults.

Defy stereotypes.

Many managers almost expect teen and new graduate job seekers to be less professional, and even less respectful, than older applicants. Show them you're different. Arrive on time to the interview. Shake hands firmly. A suit is appropriate for an interview at an office job. For more casual jobs, an ironed shirt and a nice skirt or pants are fine.

Be what the company's looking for.

Read job descriptions carefully to get a mental picture of the employer's ideal candidate. Take these two:

1. "Enthusiastic servers wanted for fast-paced, high-energy and FUN environment."

2. "Responsible individual needed for highly visible front-desk position at downtown law firm."

The smart job seeker will tailor his or her interview style to match the tone of the job description.

Naturally bubbly? Play it up for the server job (without sounding ditsy). Put on your serious face for the receptionist post (without sounding stiff and boring).

Tell them what they want to hear.

You should practice interview questions ahead of time with a friend or parent. One that you're guaranteed to hear is "**Why do you want to work here?**".

This is a trick question - it's not really about *you*, it's about the company.

Wrong answer: "Well, I think I'd enjoy working here. My friends say it's a pretty chill place."

Better answer: "I'm excited about working for one of my favourite stores and I really like the team atmosphere here."

One more classic: "**Why are you a good fit for the company?**".

Again, think about what you can offer them, not the perks they'll offer you.

Wrong answer: "I like the flexible work hours and the uniforms aren't too hideous. Besides, how could I say no to the 25% employee discount because me and my buds need a new wardrobe in time for summer?"

Better answer: "I'm a hard worker and I have a lot of energy. I think I would be a strong addition to your team."

Panel Interviews

There are some interviews where you meet with several people simultaneously. These setups are usually referred to as "panel" interviews although they seem more like a firing squad. They are usually arranged this way for one of four reasons:

a) The interviewers have limited time available so this is to convenience them.

b) There is a time constraint to hire someone so they figure that they will get it done quicker this way,

c) They don't want to inconvenience you by having you come back 4 or 5 times to meet with each interviewer separately. Or...

d) It is set up to see how well you can communicate in times of stress. Those interviews tend to involve more rapid fire questioning where each question would be asked by a different interviewer.

Don't let these interviews stress you out. These types of interviews are more typical in technical positions or roles where you would need to interact with several teams. Usually, you are notified in advance if more than 2 people would be attending the interview.

Disastrous Moments

> *"Would you like me to give you a formula for success?*
> *It's quite simple, really. Double your rate of failure.*
> *You are thinking of failure as the enemy of success. But it isn't at all. You*
> *can be discouraged by failure or you can learn from it, so go ahead and*
> *make mistakes. Make all you can.*
> *Because remember that's where you will find success."*
> *– Thomas J. Watson*

Exercise: Avoidance

Each of the ten situations shown below is best avoided in a job interview as they are likely to create the wrong impression (see statement 'a' for each situation).

If your reasons for not "performing" properly are those stated at 'b' or 'c', what would be the best way of "saving" the situation?

1. Didn't have a good reason for wanting the job.

   a) Doesn't really care about getting the job.

   b) I had one, but it came out wrong.

   c) I've run out of reasons after applying for so many jobs.

2. Didn't have sensible questions ready to ask.

   a) Doesn't show interest in the job or firm.

   b) Couldn't think of them at the right time.

   c) Lost my list of questions somewhere.

3. Didn't bring along the originals of documents.

   a) Careless - might be hiding something?

   b) I was in a big rush and I just forgot.

   c) Spilt coffee over everything at breakfast.

4. Didn't find out much about the job or firm beforehand.

   a) Not really interested in working for us.

   b) I tried but couldn't find out much.

   c) Oops... I didn't realize that I could have.

5. Doesn't answer questions well.

    a)   Not well prepared. . . doesn't care about job.

    b)   I have trouble getting my thoughts organized.

    c)   I'm not too good talking to strangers. I'm shy.

6. Didn't ask any questions.

    a)   Either poorly prepared or a 'know-it-all'.

    b)   I should've - the interview is also for me to find out if the job is suitable to me.

    c)   I had them ready, but I was too nervous to ask them.

7. Just answered YES/NO to all my questions.

    a)   Seemed bored, couldn't start a conversation.

    b)   I thought they only wanted a YES/NO answer.

    c)   It was difficult to give more than a YES/NO answer the way those questions were asked.

8. Couldn't get my name right.

    a)   Stupid so-and-so. . . what's so hard about Schmechenheimer?

    b)   I tried hard but I just couldn't get it right.

    c)   I couldn't work out what it was when I was introduced.

9. Kept asking me about the same things all the time.

    a)   Can't they remember what they're told?

    b)   I had trouble understanding what was said.

    c)   I was still unclear on a few things.

10. Always spoke very softly-didn't speak up.

    a)   Very quiet person . . . is that what we want?

    b)   I'm naturally a quiet person.

    c)   I wasn't confident enough to say what I thought.

Possible "saves" you may want to consider

Interviewer's thought	Possible save
1. Didn't have a good reason for wanting the job.	As the interview comes to a close, re-state why you are interested in the job and why you are a good fit.
2. Didn't have sensible questions ready to ask.	Tell the interview that s/he did a great job of addressing your questions before you had the chance to ask them.
3. Didn't bring along the originals of documents.	Let the interviewer know that you are happy to forward originals by end of day.
4. Didn't find out much about the job or firm beforehand.	Ask them what a typical day in the life of an employee in this company/role is. Doesn't make up for not doing research but it may show that you are interested in the company.
5. Doesn't answer questions well.	Send a "recovery" letter which is really a "thank you" letter but answers the questions you may have messed up without actually mentioning that you messed up.
6. Didn't ask any questions.	Ask if you may contact the interviewer afterwards if you have any follow-up questions.
7. Just answered YES/NO to all my questions.	Ask if there is anything that they would like you to elaborate on.
8. Couldn't get my name right.	Ask for a business card so you may contact him/her if you have any questions and then write a thank you letter directly to that person using their name in the letter.
9. Had to repeat questions to get answers I was looking for.	Ask if there is anything that you can clarify. If you don't understand the question, you can ask them to rephrase it or clarify.
10. Always spoke very softly - didn't speak up.	Shake hands firmly, smile and make direct eye contact at the end of the interview. Tell them that you are very excited about the opportunity and why you are a good fit.

Proper Business Attire for Women

When women entered the workplace in the 1970's and 1980's in greater numbers than ever before and began to move into positions which had traditionally been held by men, many of them believed that they needed to imitate male business attire. The result was women showing up at the office in skirted suits or coordinated skirts and jackets with tailored blouses finished off with an accessory item that looked very much like a man's tie. Those days are gone. While the business woman may now wear pants to work (yes, there were times when pants were not allowed), she does it out of a desire to appear professional and at the same time enjoy the flexibility and comfort that pants offer over skirts. Her goal is no longer to mirror her male colleagues.

The same overall rules apply to women's work attire as apply to men's. Business clothing is not a reflection of the latest fashion trend. A woman should be noticed for who she is and her professional skills rather than what she wears. Her business wear should be appropriate for her industry and her position or title within the industry.

Start with a skirted suit or pants suit for the most conservative look. A skirted suit is the most professional. With a few exceptions, dresses do not offer the same credibility unless they are accompanied by matching jackets.

Skirts should be knee-length or slightly above or below. Avoid extremes. A skirt more than two inches above the knee may raise eyebrows and questions.

Pants should break at the top of the foot or shoe. While capri pants that come in assorted lengths from mid-calf to ankle might be the latest trend, they are out of place in the conservative (bank, insurance company, customer facing company) business environment. They may be acceptable on a "casual Friday" or more casual work environment (software development, media); however, do not make this assumption. Better to err on the side of conservatism. Observe your co-workers over time to see what is acceptable before wearing a more relaxed wardrobe. Be sure that the people that are respected are wearing the more casual attire.

Blouses and sweaters provide range and style to a woman's clothing, but they should be appealing rather than revealing. Inappropriate necklines and waistlines can give the wrong impression. And please ensure that it is the correct size (i.e. too tight will not earn you respect or friends).

Faces, not feet, should be the focal point in business so choose conservative shoes. A low heel is more professional than high heels. In spite of current fashion, sandals or open-toed are not always considered office attire. If it is accepted in your company (check with the dress code, not the person in the next cubicle), make sure that your feet are well-maintained. Pedicures are recommended even if you don't get one done by a professional.

When it comes to accessories and jewellery, less is more. Keep it simple: one ring per hand, one earring per ear. Accessories should reflect your personality, not diminish your credibility.

Business attire is different from weekend and evening wear. Investing in a good business wardrobe is an investment in your professional future. For those who think it's not what you wear but who you are that creates success, give that some more thought. Business skills and experience count, but so does personal appearance and that all-important first impression. If you cannot afford proper business attire, check out organizations that assist women with discounted used clothing such as "Dress For Success".

Do

Don't even think about it

If you are going to an interview and you are unsure, always err on the conservative side (i.e. wear a traditional suit). You should never feel out of place if you are in a suit and your interviewers are more casually dressed. It demonstrates respect. You will feel out of place if you go to an interview more casual than the interviewer(s). This situation will guarantee a negative response from your interviewer(s).

Proper Business Attire for Men

In business, your clothing and grooming should not distract. Rather, they should direct attention to your face and particularly your eyes. When you connect with someone else's eyes, they tend to listen.

Typical formal business attire has an advantage because it can easily direct listeners to your eyes. A light shirt under a closed dark business jacket forms a "V" that opens toward the face. A contrasting tie can heighten this effect. Wearing some red in the tie can help draw the eyes of your audience to your own.

In contrast, a flashy belt buckle can draw the eye to the waist. Bright buttons, shiny tie tacks, colourful lapel pins, big metal watches, or other conspicuous jewellery can distract the eye. The same goes for clothing that is tight, shiny, or loud in colour or design flare.

When you're in front of a group giving a presentation, making a speech or just plain talking, you need to choose your attire to match the event. For example, you will typically want to dress one notch of formality above your audience. That means if they're wearing slacks and shirts, you may want to add a sports jacket to your outfit. On the other hand, wearing a suit and tie in front of an audience in jeans and T-shirts is rarely a good idea outside of a job interview.

Here's a simple test you can take before choosing attire for an event that puts you in the spotlight.

Ask yourself:

?   What's appropriate for this audience? This event?

?   What image do I want to project?

?   For my company?

?   For my department?

?   For myself?

Do

Don't even think about it

After the Interview

Interviewing can be an exhausting experience whether you felt you performed well or not. While the experience is fresh in your mind, you should try to do the following:

✓ Write down some notes on the questions asked and where you thought you did well or poorly. This will help you prepare for future interviews. Remember not to focus on the "poorly" section. All interviews, regardless of the outcome, are positive experiences in the long run.

✓ Send a "thank you" letter/email to the interviewer(s) thanking them for their time and reminding them that you are still interested in the job. Do this within a day or two of the interview and be sure that you spell the interviewer's name correctly! (See below on how to do this.)

✓ If you feel that you failed somewhere in the interview and would like the chance to readdress it, you can write a "**recovery**" letter/email. This letter is similar to the "thank you" letter but also subtly gives answers to areas in the interview that you feel you could have answered better. Remember to be sure that you would benefit by rehashing the topic. You may see this issue as bigger than it was and your letter will just remind the interviewer of your weaknesses.

✓ Don't forget to follow-up by contacting the organization if you have not heard anything from them by the date that they agreed to contact you.

✓ If you don't get the job, consider calling the interviewer for some feedback about the interview: Did I seem adequately prepared? Was there something that I did not demonstrate? How could I do better in a future interview?

Don't get discouraged! Interviews are about both parties finding the right fit for the job. Performing better in interviews is something that can be developed through preparation and practice.

Thank You Letter/Email Guidelines

- The letter has to be sent before the decision to hire a particular candidate has been made.

- It is your last opportunity to mention any information you missed to mention in your résumé, cover letter or interview.

- Clear up any misunderstandings.

- You can use some things you learnt during your interview to your advantage.

- This shows you are a professional.

- Your last opportunity to leave a good impression.

- Send it within one day of the interview.

When to use a Thank You Letter/Email :

- After an employment interview.
- To a person or contact who referred to a particular job.

Thank You Letter/Email Structure

- Short and simple is the key.
- Mention specific points discussed.

First paragraph:

In this opening paragraph, tell your interviewer that you enjoyed meeting them and provide a brief summary of your conversation with them. During your interview, make sure to note one or two things of which you spoke with this person so that you can refer back to it during the letter. For example, "I thought your method of tracking customer satisfaction was particularly interesting" or "I enjoyed hearing about your point of view regarding the challenges of the role". This is where you make certain that you personalize the time you spent with that individual.

Second paragraph:

Take the job description and make one or two comparisons to your background to highlight you are a good match for the position. You may say something like "I believe my MBA and five years of experience in Financial Analysis in the Marketing industry makes me an excellent match for your requirements to track brand revenue".

If this is also a recovery letter, this is an opportunity for you to readdress any important issue that you feel that you may have answered insufficiently. Make sure that the issue is important enough to revisit and that you won't be reminding the interviewer of something that was not an issue during the interview.

Third paragraph:

State your interest in the position and what excites you about it. Let them know that you welcome any further interviews and if they need more information to contact you.

Last paragraph:

Thank them again and say that you look forward to hearing back from them regarding the next steps.

Other tips:

Do's	Don'ts
Do use these follow-up techniques to continue to show your enthusiasm and desire for the position.	**Don't** make it seem as though you are desperate.
Do obtain the correct titles and names of all the people who interviewed you. (Ideally, do get each person's business card.)	**Don't** assume you can be overly familiar with your interviewer(s) i.e. calling "Robert" by "Bobby" if you haven't been allowed to.
Do write individual thank you's to each person who interviewed you within two business days. Each letter can be essentially the same, but try to vary each a bit in case recipients compare notes. And do write thank you notes after *every* interview.	**Don't** ever fail to send a thank you -- even if you are sure the job is not for you.
In your thank you letter, **do** show appreciation for the employer's interest in you and do remind the employer about why you are the perfect person for the position.	**Don't** ever have any errors (misspellings or typos) in your thank you letters.
Do alert your references -- if you have not done so already -- that they may be getting a phone call from the employer.	**Don't** forget to let your references know what job you are applying for and who to expect a call from.
Do continue to interview and attempt to find other opportunities.	**Don't** stop job-hunting, even if you feel confident that you will get a job offer.
Do follow-up with a telephone call to the employer within a week to ten days (or sooner, if the employer had a shorter timetable) to ask about the position. And do continue to build rapport and sell your strengths during the phone call.	**Don't** be too pushy or annoy the employer but bombarding the interviewer with calls.
Do be patient. The hiring process often takes longer than the employer expects.	**Don't** assume that no response means that they hired someone else.
Do continue following-up, especially if the employer asks you to. Remember the adage about the squeaky wheel getting the oil.	Just **don't** go overboard and annoy or bother the employer.
Do continue to look for other opportunities while you are waiting for the results of this interview. You wouldn't want to miss out on a better opportunity while you end up with a rejection on this one.	**Don't** place too much importance on one job or one interview; there will be other opportunities for you.

Samples:

7 Apple Court
Markham, ON L9L 7L4

Dr. Steven Page
Richmond Hill School Health Clinic
5 Main Street
Richmond Hill, ON L9M 4M1

Dear Dr. Page:

Thank you so much for taking the time to interview me today for the Social Worker position.

I felt a wonderful rapport not only with you, but with the entire Richmond Hill School Health Clinic staff. I am more convinced than ever that I will fit in beautifully as a member of the team and contribute my skills and talents for the benefit of school children in the Richmond Hill district.

I can make myself available for any further discussions of my qualifications that may be needed.

Again, Dr. Page, I very much appreciate you and your staff taking so much time to talk with me about this exciting opportunity.

Sincerely,

John Oakley
905.555.0303
Johnoak343@gmail.com

Dear Mr. Moody:

Thanks for taking the time to meet with me about the Account Executive position yesterday. The job seems like a very good match for my skills and interests. The strategies you outlined are just my style and I know I would hit the ground running.

In addition to my 8 years of experience in your industry, I will bring strong writing and leadership skills as well as a ton of energy to your team. I've also got solid organizational skills and know I could help bring order to the areas you mentioned.

I am very interested in working for you and look forward to hearing from you soon.

Sincerely,

Recovery letter/email sample:

Mr. James Gleeson
Midnight Widgets Inc.
756 Centre Street
Edmonton, AB T3B 5T4

Dear Mr. Gleeson,

Thank you for taking the time on Monday to interview me for the Accounting position.

I am very impressed with Midnight Widgets Inc., from both a business and cultural standpoint. It is obvious to me that Midnight Widgets has earned its excellent reputation in both the industry and the community and I would be proud to be a part of it.

You mentioned in our interview that the ability to "hit the ground running" is critical for the person you hire. If past experience is any indication, I have noted a few of my accomplishments at former employers below.

There is no question I will do the same for you.

Shadow Gadgets Ltd.
In my first 60 days in the position, I decreased the Accounts Receivables that were outstanding from 35% of total billings to 15%.

Black Consulting
In my initial 90 days, I enhanced team productivity by 15% and reduced errors by 25% by automating the month-end reporting process.

The Dallas Group
In my first year, I produced 2% annual savings by negotiating discounts with vendors and realized 50% annual savings by securing a new phone and internet provider.

I hope the above information is helpful and I look forward to taking the next step.

If you have any questions please don't hesitate to call me at 902.555.5309.

Best regards,

Jan Brady
Janfbrady555@gmail.com

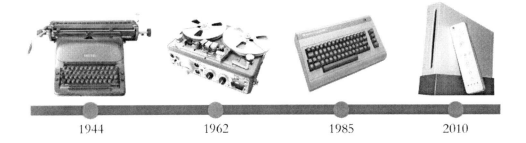

1944   1962   1985   2010

From WWII to Wii

"Each generation imagines itself to be more intelligent than the one that went before it, and wiser than the one that comes after it."
– George Orwell

Currently, there are four generations participating in the workforce. There has never been so much age diversity interacting with each other in the workplace. This situation can pose challenges for each generation. Each group has their own unique perspectives which will inherently affect their ability to communicate with each other and often causes misunderstandings and false biases.

What does this mean for you? You need to realize that the way *you* communicate may be different from the way other generations communicate. Therefore, it is essential for you to identify these differences so that you can land that job you want and succeed. While there is no doubt that you have many talents and experiences that are valuable to the company that will hire (or has hired) you, they will never be able to identify these talents if they don't understand you. And if they don't understand you, you will never be hired or promoted.

Let's start with recognizing your generation. The newest generation to join the workforce is the Millennial generation (aka "Generation Y" or" Generation Next", or" Nintendo Generation" or" Nexters", etc.). In general, you grew up with structured social interactions i.e. daycare, camps, after school programs. You are technically savvy, natural collaborators, value freedom and instant communication and positive feedback. An identifying characteristic is that you are also known to "earn to spend", that is, you work so that you can afford to play.

Sounds great? Sure it does until you compare yourself with the previous generations. You will see that the belief systems and expectations vary greatly among them.

As the average life expectancy expands and the ability to survive on pensions diminishes, the traditionalists (or "silent generation"- people born prior to 1946), still remain in the workplace. This generation is characterized as hard working, loyal, thrifty, conformist and sacrificing for the company. In most cases, these people reside in the upper levels of management.

Next comes the Baby Boomers. Born between 1946 and 1964, the Boomers are known to be competitive, moralistic, optimistic and self-focused. They were raised in the suburbs and were the first generation to have television in their homes. They tend to be workaholics and associate success with materialism. This group usually makes up a large part of management in most medium to large corporations.

The Generation X'ers , born between 1964 and 1980, are more independent and value a work-life balance. They have a strong distrust in companies and see themselves as free agents.

Comparing the Generations at a Glance

	Traditionalist Pre-1946	Baby Boomers 1946-1964	Generation Xers 1965-1980
Key descriptor(s)	Loyal	Optimistic/Competitive/Moralistic	Skeptical/Flexible
Drivers	Sense of duty	Live to work	Work to live
Notion of command	Chain of command	Change of command	Self-command
View of hierarchy	Prefer top-down; military	Comfortable with top-down	Prefer flat
What they're building	A legacy	A stellar, upward career	A portable career
Job changing	Carries a stigma	Puts you behind	Is necessary
Motivator	A job well done	Money, title, promotion	Self fulfillment, freedom, fun
Measurement of success	If still employed, then you are doing a good job	What am I achieving?	Respect on merit. Titles are irrelevant.
Workplace flexibility	Who will do the work?	The nerve of those Xers!	I'll go for the right lifestyle
Technology	Struggles with it but afraid to ask for help. Feels that direct communication is lost by technology-dependant younger generations.	Necessary Evil. Just one more thing to manage.	Comfortable.

	Traditionalists Pre -1946	Baby Boomers 1946-1964	Generation Xers 1964-1980
Working long hours	Required, prudent	Will get you ahead, money, bonus	Get a life!
Productivity	Inputs and outputs matter	Input matters most	Output is all that matters
Give me more…	Essentials	Money	Time
Performance reviews	If I'm not yelling at you, all is fine.	Once a year; well-documented	Sorry to interrupt again, how am I doing?
Work-Family	Work matters most; wife at home	Work matters most; dual career or divorced	Family matters; dual career
Career paths	Slow and steady	Ladder	Lattice
Career pace	Prove yourself with loyalty; pay dues	Prove yourself with long hours; pay dues	I want to know all my options now.
Career plan	Single career longevity rewarded (gold watch)	In 2nd or 3rd career due to layoffs. Expect to work into their 70's	Free agent with strong self focus.
Preferred office setting	Closed offices with secretaries as gate keepers	Window offices with cubicles in center of floor	Open environment
Frustrations	Youth who "think they know it all"	Lack of ambition	"Because I said so" mentality
Communication	Face-to-Face	Face-to-face or voice to voice	Immediate & electronic (texting, IM, email)

For each group, there are key messages listed below that will motivate them to your favour. Review and understand them for each group when preparing for an interview or meeting. Then, try to phrase your responses to their questions using these themes to gain their confidence.

Messages that Motivate Traditionalists

- "Your experience is respected here."
- "It's important for the rest of us to hear what has, and hasn't, worked in the past."
- "Your perseverance is valued and will be rewarded."
- Values.
- Dedication/sacrifice.
- Law and order.
- Strong work ethic.
- Risk averse.
- Respect for authority.
- Patience.
- Delayed reward.
- Duty, honor, country.
- Loyalty to the organization.
- Face-to-face skills such as presentation skills, mentoring, brainstorming and relationship building.
- "It's not like I want you to walk in the snow uphill both ways like I did, but I do want you to know what it was like for me and how I got where I did. Do not discount my experience and do not disregard me by calling me old.

Messages that Motivate Boomers

- "You are important to our success."
- "We recognize your unique and important contribution to our team."
- "What is your vision for this project?"
- "You are valued."
- Values.
- Optimism.
- Team work.
- Personal gratification.
- Health and wellness.
- Promotion and recognition.
- Work.
- Volunteerism.

Messages that Motivate Gen X'ers

- "Do it your way."
- "We've got the latest computer technology."
- "There aren't a lot of rules here."
- "We're not very corporate."
- Values.
- Diversity.
- Work needs to be meaningful.
- Thinking globally.
- Balance in life.
- Computer literacy.
- Fun.
- Creativity.
- Informality.
- Independence.
- Initiative.
- Collaboration.

So now that you have this new insight into how each group in the workplace thinks. Now, remember this is a generalization so it is possible that there will be some traditionalists who enjoy new technology and some Boomers who aren't great collaborators. However, if you keep some of these differences in mind, you are guaranteed to be more successful in your interviews or on-the-job interactions.

✎ Exercise: Generation Gap

For each of the questions below, write a possible response that would appeal to each generation. Remember to try to reflect some of the key areas of interest that are listed above. Always use examples in your responses where you have them. The example below is an illustration of a possible response but you should make sure that all your responses are in your own voice.

Example:

What would your colleagues say about you?

Traditionalist response

I am very well respected by my colleagues in part due to my loyalty, commitment, strong work ethic and ability to bring a personal touch. While many people today are well versed in electronic communication, I also have the ability to communicate effectively face-to-face whether it is presenting information to management, brainstorming with co-workers or relationship building with clients. [Add brief examples where face-to-face communication made a team work better or made someone feel at ease.] I have also gained a lot of insight from listening to the experiences of past mentors. [Add example where mentor gave you insight and how you positively utilized that.]

Boomer response

I am very well respected by my colleagues in part due to my success through teamwork and collaboration. I am able to achieve lofty targets through sheer drive and the ability to communicate effectively with people. [Add example.]

Gen-X response

I am very well respected by my colleagues in part due to my success through my ability to generate creative solutions and collaborate easily with my team. [Add example of where you showed initiative and creativity.]

Exercise: Anticipate the Responses

This exercise will get you in the mode to think how other generations think. By doing this, you will be able to anticipate how to frame your responses to interview questions if any of the interviewers are from another generation.

Anticipate the different generational responses to these questions. Try thinking of your own questions and potential responses.

Are you more energized by working with data or by collaborating with other individuals?

Traditionalist
Response:_____

Boomer
Response:_____

Gen X
Response:_____

What does success mean to you? How do you measure it?

Traditionalist
Response:_____

Boomer
Response:_____

Gen X
Response:_____

Why do you think you would do well at this job?

Traditionalist
Response:_____

Boomer
Response:_____

Gen X
Response:_____

When you do an outstanding job, how do you want to be rewarded?

Traditionalist
Response:_____

Boomer
Response:_____

Gen X
Response:_____

Describe your ideal feedback scenario. (i.e. What format? How often do you want to receive it? Who should provide it?)

Traditionalist
Response:_____

Boomer
Response:_____

Gen X
Response:_____

Describe the ideal work / life balance.

Traditionalist
Response:_____

Boomer
Response:_____

Gen X
Response:_____

Is the concept of "paying your dues" outdated?

Traditionalist
Response:_____

Boomer
Response:_____

Gen X
Response:_____

❧ Exercise: Interviewers of Different Generations

What kind of questions would you ask the interviewer depending on his/her generational fit? Would you ask different questions or just adjust the phrasing of the questions? Make sure that the question(s) also show you in a positive light while addressing what your interviewer is looking to hear. Write down some questions for each generation.

Example:

Traditionalist
What is the organization's plan for the next five years, and how does this department fit in?

Boomer
What would be a surprising but positive thing the new person could do in first 90 days?

Gen X
Can you tell me a little bit about the team [or technology] that I will be working with most closely?

Now you try it.

Traditionalist
Question(s):_____

_____

_____

_____

Boomer
Question(s):_____

_____

_____

_____

Gen X
Question(s):_____

_____

_____

_____

Final question:

What do you do if you are interviewed by a panel that consists of a compilation of various generations? Ideally, you would try to tailor your answers to satisfy each need with subtlety. Don't be too obvious that you are doing this. You want to be seen as having integrity and confidence in your abilities. As well, you want to be consistent in your answers. For example, if you are answering a question that is focused on communication style, you need to be careful that your response does not start with your preference for email (good answer for GenX but not for Traditionalist) and then turn to the Traditionalist interview and state that you prefer face-to-face. In that situation, you may want to express that you are equally comfortable in both styles and use examples where you used each to effective results.

However, you may want to emphasize one generation's motivators based on which generation is asking the question. But be sure that you are not saying what the questioner wants to hear to the exclusion of the other panel members. Many times, panel members will split up questions regardless of who wrote them.

What to Expect on the Job

"The artist is nothing without the gift,
but the gift is nothing without work."
-- Emile Zola

Now that you have gotten the job, the hard work and stress is over, right? Wrong!

In order to be successful, make sure that you understand what is expected of you and meet (or exceed) those expectations.

Your Expectations as an Employee

Firstly, let's start with your needs. There are certain behaviours you can expect from the company you work for. You can expect your employer to:

- Pay your salary.

- Provide safe working conditions.

- Provide some training related to the specific needs of your job.

- Provide reasonable accommodation for disability related needs.

- Explain company policies, rules and regulations.

- Tell you about changes in your duties, responsibilities, working relationships, rate of pay, vacation schedule, etc.

- Evaluate your work by telling you both the positive and negative aspects of your performance in a private setting.

If you believe that your new employer is not meeting these expectations, schedule a meeting with your supervisor to discuss your concerns.

Your Employer's Expectations of You

As a new hire, there are certain behaviours/characteristics the company will expect from you as an employee. Listed below are expectations the employer will have for you as an employee.

Initiative

Employers will expect you to complete your own job and if you haven't been told what to do, look around to see what needs to be done and do it. Don't wait to be asked!

Willingness to Learn

Your employer will expect you to learn the way things are done in the company.

Willingness to Follow Directions

Always follow directions exactly as you are told.

Honesty

Employers will expect you to be honest and to tell the truth. Other forms of dishonesty on the job are: starting work late, leaving work early and stealing company property. Stealing time is the most costly form of dishonesty on the job. You "steal" time when you come in late or leave early, make personal calls (even if it is on your own cell phone) or surf the internet during work time that has not been designated as "break time".

Dependability

Your employer will expect you to be on the job every day and on time. If you will be absent or late, you must call your supervisor. If you have an appointment with your doctor, dentist, etc. let your supervisor know in advance. Try to make appointments before or after work so you won't lose time from your job.

Enthusiasm

The most successful employees are those who are enthusiastic about their work.

Acceptance of Criticism

Criticism is the way a supervisor tells you how they want a job done. You are expected to improve because of it. Listen and learn from the constructive criticisms your supervisor will share with you. Make sure that you understand exactly what is expected. Try to see how it can help you become a better worker. Even if you feel the criticism is unfair, try not to lose your temper. Do not take it personally. It is about your current performance in the office, not your value as a human being.

Punctuality

Arrive at work on time and don't leave early.

Dress Appropriately

Dress the way your co-workers do.

Ask for Further Instructions

If the task is unclear or if you are unsure how to complete an assignment before it is due, request clarification. Don't wait until it is due and say that you didn't understand.

Be Flexible

Accept assignments that may not fall under your specified job duties because of time and/or staff constraints.

Observe and Respect Chain of Command

Learn what positions each of your co-workers holds in the office and how their positions relate to yours.

Understand Deadlines

If you find that you cannot meet a deadline, please notify the appropriate person as soon as possible with reasons and an attainable new deadline. Understand the impact that your new deadline will have on your co-workers and customers. Don't wait until the deadline has passed!

Able to Generate Ideas

Someone who is creative and innovative can be an asset and a liability at the same time. In one way, every manager would love to have a team member who can come up with new ideas and concepts. However, such people are often treated as strange as they think off-the-beaten-path and other people are uncomfortable with that type of talent. They fear that you either can't conform or are looking for glory.

Willing to Collaborate

It is not uncommon for team members to be resistant to collaboration. Many people feel incorrectly that hoarding information leads to job security. Actually, it is quite the opposite. If you choose to be the sole custodian of key knowledge, your team members will resent you and your manager will isolate you. More importantly, you will marginalize your promotion opportunities as your manager cannot allow you to progress up the ladder if you withhold key information.

Stay Current

Don't just isolate yourself from on what goes on in the office. Make sure that you understand what goes on in the world not just your company. Events in the world not only affect you but also your company, industry, marketplace, customers and competition.

Be the Driver of Your Development

Don't wait for your employer to suggest courses or developmental activities. You are responsible for your own career. Formal training is not the only venue for education. Try mentors or peers willing to give you their time. Request assignments that are out of your comfort zone. You may struggle at first but it is the willingness to face a challenge that will get you noticed and expand your knowledge, regardless of the result.

Ride the Rollercoaster

It is easy to be a star player during a winning season for the company or department; however, can you be one during times of decline? Can you demonstrate all of the behaviours listed above during tough times? It is key (although difficult) to keep motivated and positive when events indicate a downturn. As the old adage says, there are no problems, just opportunities.

When someone offers to help you, accept the assistance pleasantly and with a smile. But don't depend too much on others because they have their own jobs to do.

If someone asks for your help, **never** say "That is not my job". It is good to share unpleasant tasks (duties) because sharing is important in working relationships. Also, remember if your work is finished, you can offer to help someone else. Sharing work helps to build good relationships.

When in doubt, ask questions. Don't hesitate. When you need help, ask for it. But when you are sure of what you are doing, do it. People will respond to you if you let them know you want to learn and want to work.

What Employers are Really Looking For

There's a common list of skills and requirements for employees. This section discusses the traits that make a great employee and those that are sure ways to get fired. These are true, not only for teens, but for all workers young and old in any field. After reading through this section, the things your teachers are teaching you in school might make more sense.

Hardworking

This would seem obvious, but people are fired for being lazy.

Ellen was a lazy student in school. When she passed a class, it was barely. Ellen promised herself when she got a job her lethargic ways would change. Ellen was lucky enough to interview with an employer that didn't ask about her grades. She got and started the job but she and her employer discovered that habits can be extremely hard to break. She was fired because she didn't have a good work ethic.

Dependability

Most often this is tied to lateness and absences without justification. Attendance issues are one of the top things people are fired for in this country. Businesses are strict; much stricter than your school when it comes to attendance. In order for an employer to benefit from your work, you have to be there, as well as perform effectively.

Drew couldn't seem to make it to work on time. He was never more than 8 minutes late, but the company he worked for had a very strict policy. A note went into his file after he was late two times, which meant he received no annual bonus. After his 4th*, he was fired.*

If you don't already use a planner or a PDA calendar, you need to start. Don't depend on memory to keep track of school, work schedules and all your other activities. It will get to be too much. As a part-time worker, your schedule could be different from one week to the next. To avoid costly mistakes, always write things down.

Dependability also has to do with doing what you said you would, when you said you would do it. As you mature, more and more people will depend on you. If you want to be taken seriously, you can't gap-out physically or mentally and leave people hanging.

Responsibility

Self-motivated people are mature people. They are also the people who can make decisions and stand behind those decisions, good or bad. If you screw up, the fault belongs to you (not anybody else) so don't complain about your mistakes. Learn from them.

Monica's employer knew his young employees would make mistakes. What he didn't expect was his difficulty discussing those mistakes with Monica. Each time he tried to teach her something about her job she interrupted him to explain why her mistake was someone else's fault. This irritated her employer and her fellow employees until he was forced to let Monica go.

In school, being responsible is really a suggestion. In reality, there's not a lot that educators can do if you decide to do nothing. In the world of work, employees must be responsible. If you cannot meet that expectation, you will simply not have a job.

Honesty and Integrity

This topic is rather clear and simple. Having these qualities is a basic prerequisite that all employers expect. If these two fundamental qualities are missing from your character set, then please don't get a job because you give all younger applicants a bad name.

Flexibility and Willingness

Adapting to new situations and things you are asked to do is important. You are going into an entry-level position, which means you will do some things that you don't like to do. We've all been there! Ask your parents about their first jobs. Have the ability to be willing and flexible in your job. Do the things you don't necessarily want to. Pay your dues and someday you won't be at the bottom. Flipping burgers should never be beneath your dignity. Your grandparents had a different word for burger flipping; they called it "opportunity".

Dylan was hired as a receptionist in a dentist's office. He wasn't told when he was hired that one of his responsibilities was to clean the bathroom. Dylan refused when his boss told him to grab a toilet brush and get busy. He stated, "That's not what I was hired to do." Dylan quit that job, but found that no matter where he went to work, he was expected to do tasks he didn't necessarily care for.

Respectful

Without respect for others, you can't get along in the workplace. Inability to show respect in the workplace shares the top spot with a lack of dependability for the reason why people are fired. All jobs require you to be a member of a team. The team can only be successful if there is respect between its members. As you've probably been told a number of times, you can't get respect until you give it.

Bill knew printing machines very well. When his employer gave Bill and his fellow employees a big project to do, he emphasized the need to work as a team in order to meet the deadline. Bill didn't have respect for the others' ability to get things done. Bill tried to take over the project himself, ignoring another employee when she pointed out a typo to Bill. He was fired when he printed ten thousand customer operating guides with a mistake on them.

Positive Attitude

You can't be depressed, mad or moody while you are at work. Many of you will be working with customers who expect a positive attitude - not to mention your fellow employees who have to be around you too. A negative attitude in the workplace is like cancer: it spreads. In order to return to health, the cancer has to be eliminated, just as the employee with the negative attitude has to be fired.

Karla was having a lot of problems at home. Instead of embracing the time at work as a time to be away and think about something else, she stewed about the issues. Karla snapped at customers and her coworkers, and generally made everyone around her tired of her attitude. When her mood became so destructive that customers began to complain about her rude behaviour, her employer fired her.

What it really comes down to is remaining an optimist rather than a pessimist. This is not an easy thing to do, particularly if there are negative things going on in your life. There are several choices you get to make on a daily basis; your attitude is one of them. For the sake of remaining employed, choose to have a positive attitude.

Life-long Learner

If you've ever read your school's mission statement, it probably includes something about creating life-long learners. What this means is that you are willing and able to learn new things throughout your life. In other words, just because you get a diploma doesn't mean you're done learning. Jobs are going to require you to keep training and keep learning and usually without the luxury of time or formal training. Otherwise, you cannot advance within your company, or in many cases, even keep your job. You have to be self-motivated and resourceful to keep up your learning so that you don't fall behind everyone else.

Being in the technology field, there is a high demand to keep up on new products and updates in the marketplace. Hired as an "expert" in the area of Peoplesoft CRM software, Judy assumed that her job would focus on what she already knows inside and out. However, had Judy signed up for Peoplesoft user groups and various CRM industry journals, she would have learned about the impending purchase of Peoplesoft by its biggest competitor, Oracle. When Judy's company announced that they would change their CRM software to Oracle within the year, Judy was angry and adamant that her school days were over even though her company offered to send her for training at no cost to her. Once the migration was complete, Judy was fired as her role was now obsolete and she refused to learn the new product.

Focus

Having Attention Deficit Disorder ("ADD") will not work as an excuse at a job. Employers need you to be able to focus and pay attention to detail. Not only is this needed for quality in your work, but it's for your safety as well. Work accidents happen when employees lose focus.

Keith was not known for his ability to listen. He tended to daydream instead. He was doing just that when his boss was explaining the company's new database system to him. When she finished, she left Keith to input customer data in a spreadsheet. He completed the task, but did it wrong. Needless to say, Keith's inability to focus lost him his job.

Learning the Corporate Culture

The corporate culture of an organization is the set of unwritten rules that dictate how the organization runs. While you are anxious to set the world on fire, as a new employee, rarely will there be someone who will teach these rules to you. Therefore, it is up to you to observe and watch the social interactions of your co-workers to see "how things are done in this office".

During your first days at the organization, keep your eyes and ears open and watch to see how the office runs. You will be evaluated not only for your work performance, as well as how well you "fit" into the company's culture. For example, you might look for the following things:

Watch how your co-workers interact with each other.

Are there certain cliques (groups) that you can see are formed? Is this an informal atmosphere where the co-workers are casual and friendly with each other? Or is it a formal atmosphere that does not tolerate much socializing?

Watch to see how your co-workers complete their assignments.

Is there a particular format or "norm" that everyone appears to follow?

Is there a chain of authority that exists depending upon a person's position within the company?

That is, as a new employee, are there certain things that you are not "supposed to do" because you would be overstepping your boundaries?

What are your co-workers' attitudes towards the Supervisor?

Does the Supervisor tend to treat all employees the same or does it appear that some employees are given favoured assignments?

What type of office politics exist in the workplace?

Are there certain unspoken policies and procedures that are followed?

Do individuals in the office tend to help one another or is work carried out independently?

Is this a competitive atmosphere, or is the management trying to promote a "family-like" environment and encourage team-work.?

Is there a person in the office who can officially or unofficially act as your mentor?

Also, can that person be someone that you can refer all your questions to, rather than having to ask your Supervisor?

Building Work Relationships:

- Networking/Meeting people is important.
- Don't forget that you are the new person.
- Try to meet people in your work area.
- It takes time! So be patient with yourself.
- Good co-worker relationships help to give you a positive image.
- Use caution when sharing personal events in your life with co-workers.
- Try to resolve problems with co-workers on your own.
- Don't talk too much about your personal life like your alcohol consumption abilities or your dating exploits. Stay professional.
- Be nice to the newer person on the job. Don't boss them around just because you aren't the newbie anymore.

Your First Career Experience

Don't be surprised if:

- This job does not satisfy <u>all</u> your personal and professional cravings.

- This job does not keep you intellectually stimulated every minute.

- This job does not use all the brains and abilities you think you have.

- This job does not guarantee instant expertise.

- You are given some mundane chores (photocopying, faxing, inputting data, etc.)

- You don't receive regular feedback.

- You rarely see your boss.

- You have to stay late sometimes.

On the other hand, you should be able to:

- Develop related career skills.

- Have the opportunity for career exploration.

- Gain personal satisfaction.

- Learn the importance of positive work attitude.

- Have the opportunity to practice thinking and observing skills.

- Improve your ability to seek and maintain employment.

Keep a list of your accomplishments (no matter how small). This will become a valuable tool when updating your résumé or justifying a promotion or salary increase down the line.

Getting Along With Your Supervisor:

- Understand that not all supervisors are the same... many different work styles and temperaments.

- Adapt to your Supervisor's way of doing things.

- Don't be upset if your Supervisor has a bad day.

- Don't "go over your Supervisor's head" without permission.

- Ask for a few minutes now and then to discuss how you are doing on the job. Be sure it is a convenient time.

- Express your appreciation and satisfaction.

- Don't let fear get in the way of a good working relationship with your Supervisor.

Resolving Conflict:

- Observe and survey the situation first!
- Ask to speak with your Supervisor or co-worker. Find an appropriate time to meet.
- Describe the situation in objective, neutral terms. Avoid accusations or negative remarks. Express your feelings using "I" statements.
- Suggest a change or compromise; remember, your idea may still not be accepted!
- After all this, put the problem aside.

Start On The Right Foot

Try answering the following questions after you have been in the new setting for a few days. If you can get the answers to these questions, you'll be off to a good start!!

Who

- Who does what in your work environment?
- To whom are you responsible?
- Who are good sources for special types of information?
- Who are the "important" people?
- Who are the people who are destined to succeed?
- Which people are well-connected or have management's ear?

What

- What are your responsibilities?
- What specific tasks are you expected to do by yourself, with co-workers or with your Supervisor?
- What, if any, office policies should you know? List them and check with your Supervisor to clarify, if necessary.

How

- How does the work get done?
- Do individuals help one another, or is work carried our independently?
- Are you expected to seek instructions frequently or is your work reviewed as you work?
- How do you get in touch with the right person in case you are sick, or some emergency comes up?
- How do you get the resources you need?

Where

- Where are important items kept?
- Where can answers be found? (Ask questions about such details. People like to keep new-comers informed.)
- Where do you fit into the organizational chart?

When

- When are deadlines for work assignments?
- When is the appropriate time to ask questions?

"As you climb the ladder of success, check occasionally to make sure it is leaning against the right wall."
- Anonymous

Working Abroad

Pay your way and get work experience by working while travelling. Canada has formal agreements with many countries to allow youth to work there temporarily. Those countries include:

Australia
Austria
Belgium
Chile
Czech Republic
Denmark
France
Germany
Ireland

Italy
Japan
Korea
Latvia
Netherlands
New Zealand
Norway
Sweden
Switzerland

Canada also has youth mobility arrangements with the United States and the United Kingdom. Several non-profit development and educational organizations also sponsor Canadian youth to work abroad.

Find out what it takes, as a Canadian, to set-up a work term abroad. Be aware that depending on the country involved, **you may need to:**

- Pay for your own travel, food and accommodation.
- Find your own job in the country that you visit.
- Be a Canadian citizen.
- Hold a valid passport.
- Get a work visa from the country that you want to visit.
- Prove that you have money to support yourself and/or a return travel ticket, plus medical and/or liability insurance.
- Prove that you have no criminal record.
- Be a student or recent graduate.
- Report your location to authorities.
- Pay a fee to obtain a work visa.

Keep in mind that the age of eligibility, length of time of the visa and ability to renew the visa will also vary from country to country. For more details, visit the web sites below.

Helpful Web Sites:

Learn about working holidays, student work abroad programs, international co-op placements and young professional / young worker opportunities through Foreign Affairs and International Trade Canada's International Youth Programs Web site (www.international.gc.ca). The site includes links to contacts for each participating country, some youth mobility agreements and links to organizations that sponsor youth to work abroad.

Prepare yourself to work abroad with "Working Abroad"

"Unravelling the maze" (http://www.voyage.gc.ca/publications/work-abroad_travail-etranger-eng.asp), a guide from Foreign Affairs and International Trade Canada that contains information on finding a job in another country, evaluating job offers, getting proper documents, insurance, health, vaccinations, housing, money and many other topics.

10 Common (Yet Wrong) Assumptions

"Don't confuse having a career with having a life"
- Hillary Clinton

10 Wrong Assumptions in Choosing a Career

Do you think you know everything about choosing a career? Many people think they know the right way to go about picking an occupation, but they often wind up choosing a career that is unsatisfying. They base their choices on their parent's expectations, their friend's expectations, society's expectations as well as their financial expectations. Here are ten assumptions about choosing a career along with resources that can help you make an informed decision.

1. Choosing a career is simple.

Actually, choosing a career is an involved process and you should give it the time it deserves. Career planning is a multi-step path that involves learning enough about yourself and the occupations which you are considering in order to make an informed decision. Oh, and plan to change your career throughout your lifetime as industries, technologies and your interests change.

2. A career counsellor can tell me what occupation to pick.

Neither a career counsellor nor any other career development professional can tell you what career is best for you. S/He can provide you with guidance in choosing a career and can help facilitate your decision. But the choice always resides with you!

3. I can't make a living from my hobby.

Says who? When choosing a career, it makes perfect sense to choose one that is related to what you enjoy doing in your spare time. In addition, people tend to become very skilled in their hobbies even though most of the skill is gained informally.

4. I should choose a career from a "Best Careers" list.

Every year, especially during milestone years, (i.e. the beginning of a new decade), there are numerous articles and books that list what "the experts" predict will be "hot jobs". It can't hurt to look at those lists to see if any of the careers on it appeal to you but you shouldn't use the list to dictate your choice.

While the predictions are often based on valid data, sometimes things change. Way too often, what is hot this year won't be hot a few years from now. In addition, you need to take into account your interests, values and skills when choosing a career. Just because the outlook for an occupation is good, it doesn't necessarily mean that occupation is right for you.

5. Making a lot of money will make me happy.

While salary is surely important, it isn't the only factor you should look at when choosing a career. Countless surveys have shown that money doesn't necessarily lead to job satisfaction. For many people enjoying what they do at work is much more important. However, you should consider earnings, among other things, when evaluating an occupation.

6. Once I choose a career, I'll be stuck in it forever.

Not true. If you are unsatisfied in your career for any reason, you can always change it. You'll be in good company. Many people change careers several times over the course of their lifetimes. It is now expected that most people entering the job market today will have 4-6 careers (not jobs but careers) in their lifetime.

7. **If I change careers, my skills will go to waste.**

Your skills are yours to keep. You can take them from one job to another. You might not use them in the exact same way but they won't go to waste.

8. **If my best friend (or sister, uncle, or neighbour) is happy in a particular field, I will be too.**

Everyone is different and what works for one person won't necessarily work for another - even if that other person is someone with whom you have a lot in common. If someone you know has a career that interests you, look into it but be aware of the fact that it may not necessarily be a good fit for you.

9. **All I have to do is pick an occupation... Things will fall into place after that.**

Choosing a career is a great start, but there's a lot more to do after that. A career plan is a road map that takes you from choosing a career to becoming employed in that occupation to reaching your long-term career goals.

10. **There's very little I can do to learn about an occupation without actually working in it.**

While first-hand experience is great, there are other ways to explore an occupation. You can read about it either in print resources or online. You can also interview those working in that field by requesting an informational interview (discussed earlier).

Invest time and research in your career as well as patience and an open mind. While your career is not set in stone, every time you change your career (and by average, we are expected to change it 4-6 times in our lifetime), you will be starting at the bottom.

Once you understand the strategy for success in the workplace, you will be on your way to a triumphant career.

"Blessed are the flexible, for they shall not be bent out of shape."
- Anonymous

Index

A

Action Words 87
Applying for a job..136
Attire
    Men 195
    Women 193

C

Corporate Culture 222
Cover letters/emails
    Body..116
    Closing 118
    Formatting & organization 119
    Heading..113
    Introduction...115
    Samples 131
    Top Mistakes 109

E

Employment gaps 100
Employment Restrictions.....................................5
Expectations
    Employee 216
    Employer...217

G

Generations in the workplace.............................203

H

Hidden job market 16

I

Inexperience .... See Résumés: Experience
Informational Meetings 17
Internet job search..20
Interviews
    After the interview 197
    Asking Questions 178
    Body language 184
    Disastrous Moments 190
    Non-verbal communication 182
    Panels 189
    Preparation 159
    Questions 164
    Red Flags 178

J

Job scams 33
Job Search 13, 15
Job websites 22

M

Misleading employment ads 29

N

Newspaper classified ads 24

O

Own business 8

P

Professional Profile .... See Résumés: Qualifications

R

Recruitment agencies..16
Résumés 37
    Chronological 83
    Contact Section 56
    Education 65
    Experience......................................45, 70
    Functional 81
    Honours & Activities 92
    Objective Statement 59
    Qualifications 62
    Samples 50, 71
    Samples - Tailored 97
    Skills 40
    Uses...48

S

Scanning résumés 21
Screening 143
Social Media
    Blog...23, 78
    Facebook 23, 78
    LinkedIn 23, 78

Twitter... 23, 78
Website 23

T

Thank you letters
    Samples.. 200

CPSIA information can be obtained at www.ICGtesting.com
Printed in the USA
LVOW092302220413

330358LV00004B/16/P

9 780986 668401

Volunteer Work

"Starting out to make money is the greatest mistake in life.
Do what you feel you have a flair for doing, and if you are
good enough at it, the money will come."
- Greer Garson

Work without pay? Yes! Volunteering may be one of the most valuable experiences of your life. It's a double win: your community or cause benefits from your work and you benefit from your experiences.

How? Read on…

Why volunteer?

Volunteering is a great way to get work experience! You learn new skills by trying new jobs. You might find something you'd like to do for a living or discover what you would not want to do.

Better yet, you can meet people who can give you guidance and possibly help you to find a paid job later on.

- Some volunteer opportunities involve travel across Canada or to other countries.
- Employers will be impressed that you took the initiative to learn new things.
- You can learn how a charitable organization works.
- Best of all, you will be taking action to promote what you think is important and probably be helping someone else along the way.

Who needs volunteers?
- Animal Shelters.
- Hospitals.
- Charities.
- Clubs.
- Overseas development organizations.
- Music and arts festivals.
- Sporting leagues and events.
- Children's camps.
- Libraries.
- Environmental organizations.
- Crisis lines and peer counselling organizations.
- Human rights organizations.
- Religious organizations.
- Political campaigns.
- Government agencies (local, provincial, federal).
- Boys & Girls Clubs.
- Elderly support organizations and homes.
- Immigration support groups.

What are some of the things a volunteer can do?
- Coach a team.
- Read to children.
- Raise money for charity (fight diseases, reduce poverty, help the sick and injured, etc.).
- Care for the elderly.
- Feed the hungry.
- Provide counselling and support.
- Run errands and do deliveries.

- Gather and analyze data.
- Raise awareness of important issues.
- Do clean-up and repairs in the community.
- Build houses or playground equipment.
- Care for animals.
- Stage concerts, plays and other cultural events.
- Protect the environment.
- Plant trees.
- Help-out with a political campaign.

Where can you find volunteer opportunities?

- Visit your community's volunteer bureau, community information centre, or town hall.
- Call a service club.
- Visit a hospital.
- Ask family, friends and neighbours what they recommend.
- Join an organization whose activities you support.
- Consult the web sites of major volunteer organizations - some can be found through www.charityvillage.ca
- Research local volunteer requirements online – Google is a great place to start.
- Research the web site of any company that you would like to work for and check out their "Community Sponsorship" page. See what community organizations that the company supports and volunteer with that charity group. It will not only give you excellent experience but it will look great on your résumé when you apply to that company.